The Coastside Trail Guidebook

- Plants • Animals • Historical Lore

- Half Moon Bay

- San Mateo County Coast

New and Expanded Edition

Barbara VanderWerf

Gum Tree Lane Books
El Granada, California

The Coastside Trail Guidebook

ISBN: 0-9632922-3-4
Library of Congress Catalog Card Number: 94-073266
Printed and bound in the United States of America

The following people and agencies made the Coastside Trail possible:

John and Terry Hernandez
Barbara VonGlahn

Carol Nelson, District Superintendent, San Mateo Coast District,
    California Department of Parks and Recreation.
Therese Ambrosi Smith, Director of Parks and Recreation,
    City of Half Moon Bay.
Peter Callander, Callander Associates, San Mateo.

Metropolitan Transportation Commission
California Coastal Conservancy
Peninsula Community Foundation
California Department of Parks and Recreation
City of Half Moon Bay
San Mateo County Harbor District,
    Donald F. Guluzzi, General Manager

My thanks go to Shirley Zynda of Half Moon Bay, who shared her research on
Sweetwood Park, to Ken Lajoie, geologist at US Geological Survey Menlo Park,
who shared his research on shoreline erosion, and to Dan Robinson of Pacifica for
information about World War II on the Coastside.

Also, thank you to those keen observers—Bill, Joel and Martha.

Photos courtesy of—
    Randolph Brandt Collection (Courtesy Tom Gray)—pages 32 (top), 45.
    Louie Bertolucci —pages 16, 53 (top), 60 (both), 61.
    Liz Hastings Collection (Courtesy Kai Tiura)—pages 10, 44 (top).
    Liz Hastings Collection (Courtesy Carol and Collin Tiura)—page 59.
    Ken Lajoie, USGS—page 43.
    Vernon Sappers—page 102 (top).
    San Mateo County Harbor District—page 29.
    Will Whittaker—page 101.

Gum Tree Lane Books
P.O. Box 1574
El Granada, CA 94018

Contents

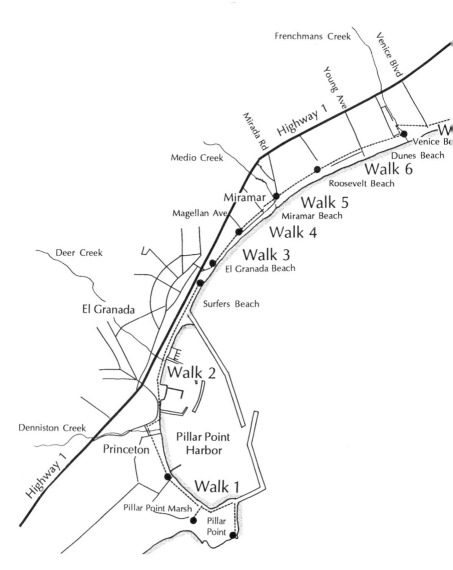

Frenchmans Creek

Venice Blvd

Young Ave

Highway 1

Mirada Rd

Medio Creek

Venice Be

Dunes Beach

Walk 6

Roosevelt Beach

Miramar

Walk 5

Magellan Ave

Miramar Beach

Walk 4

Deer Creek

Walk 3

El Granada Beach

El Granada

Surfers Beach

Walk 2

Denniston Creek

Pillar Point Harbor

Highway 1

Princeton

Walk 1

Pillar Point Marsh

Pillar Point

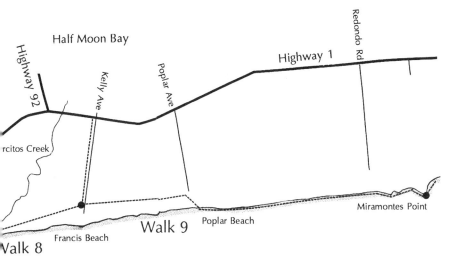

The Coastside Trail

Nine easy walks along Half Moon Bay
between Pillar Point and Miramontes Point
on the San Mateo County coast.

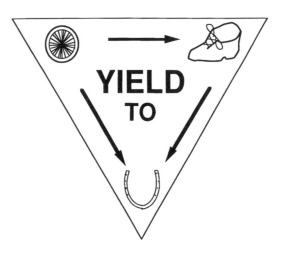

Courtesy Along the Coastside Trail

Please keep pets on leashes.

Bicyclists keep to the right except when passing. Please call out to walkers when you pass.

Riding stable horses can use the Coastside Trail south of Frenchmans Creek only.

Private horses can use the Coastside Trail north of Frenchmans Creek. Please ride in single file and keep to the edge of the trail.

Bicyclists and walkers: Yield to horseback riders at all times.

Please—no motorized vehicles except motorized wheelchairs.

Plants and animals are protected along the Coastside Trail.

Introduction

The Coastside Trail along the shore of Half Moon Bay is one trail you don't want to miss. Where else can you enjoy six miles of easy walking and biking along the Pacific Ocean?

From the trail, you can explore Pillar Point Harbor, relics of the old Ocean Shore Railroad, and protected tidepools and marsh lands. You can observe the ocean gobbling the shoreline and native plants reconquering abandoned vegetable fields. You can watch winter storms pile up offshore; enjoy wildflowers bobbing in the spring winds; stand beneath dripping eucalyptus trees in the summer fogs; and bask in the warm fall sunshine.

Who uses the Coastside Trail? Here's who—parents with children in strollers and on training bicycles, walkers, joggers, bicycle riders, horseback riders, people in wheelchairs, kids carrying surfboards looking for the perfect wave, people walking dogs on leashes, bird watchers, and couples arm-in-arm who stop to chat with friends made on the trail.

Coastsiders for Safe Bikeways: Over seven years ago, Coastsiders for Safe Bikeways had a vision: to provide a safe trail along the San Mateo County coast for bicycle riders, walkers and horseback riders. Today, after much hard work and with the help of supporting agencies, much of their vision is a reality.

• For more information, please contact Parks and Recreation, City of Half Moon Bay at (415) 726-8297.

California Coastal Trail: The Coastside Trail is part of the California Coastal Trail, which eventually will run between the Mexican border and the Oregon state line.

• For more information, please contact Coastwalk, 1389 Cooper Road, Sebastopol, CA 95472.

Happy Exploring!

The Coastside Trail Guidebook is divided into nine walks. Each walk is between one-quarter mile and three-quarters mile long. For each walk, the *Guidebook* includes a trail map and lists the availability of parking, bathrooms, drinking water, beach access, benches and wheelchair access to the trail.

Walk 1

Pillar Point and Pillar Point Marsh

Distance: Three-quarters mile one way.
Parking: Pillar Point Marsh.
Beach access: Yes.
Bathrooms: Yes.
Water: No.
Wheelchair access: Yes.
Directions: From the stop light on Highway One, take Capistrano Road to Pillar Point Harbor. Continue past the harbor entrance to Prospect Way. Turn left, then right on Broadway, then immediately left on Harvard. Continue to the end of Harvard. Turn right on West Point. Go 0.5 mile to the Pillar Point Marsh parking lot.

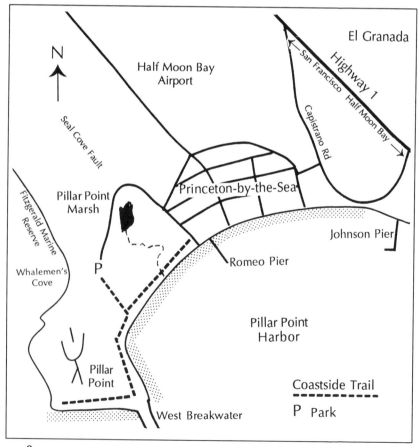

To enjoy the best Coastside bird watching and beachcombing, take a leisurely stroll around Pillar Point.

Pillar Point

No one can hike on the Coastside without being aware of Pillar Point, the promontory which dominates the northern shore of Half Moon Bay. During the day, sunlight plays across its steep cliffs. At night, the lights of the Air Force Tracking Station form a backdrop to the lights of Pillar Point Harbor. In the summer, fog first rolls over its ridge before blanketing the rest of the Coastside. In the winter, storms can blast 90-mile-an-hour winds across the tracking antennas. (In December of 1967, the winds were strong enough to blow the original dish antenna over the cliff to the rocks below.)

Sturdy Pillar Point created Half Moon Bay. For thousands of years, waves out of the northwest have bent around its rugged cliffs to carve out a perfect half-moon from the land behind. It is no wonder that to many folks, Pillar Point is THE defining landscape feature of the Coastside.

Names

Fortunately, the name Snake's Head never took hold for Pillar Point, even though its diamond shape suggested that name to the first American ranchers. The Spanish called the point "El Pillar." By the late 1860s, everyone said Pillar Point.

In 1910, no structures stood on Pillar Point and no breakwater enclosed a harbor in Half Moon Bay.

All the people who have lived along the shores of Half Moon Bay have used Pillar Point. For thousands of years, Native American Costanos gathered shellfish at its base. Their old shell midden lies hidden deep in the marsh. From the 1790s through the 1890s, Spaniards, Mexicans and Americans grazed long-horned cattle on its ridge. In the 1860s, Portuguese whalers sighted passing Humpback Whales from its high point and then launched their whaling boats from Whalemen's Cove just below. Beachcombers still find fragments of whale bones in the sand. In the 1920s and 30s, Coastside farmers grew artichokes and peas on its crown. But no one built any structures on its windswept heights.

Pillar Point: The Instrumentation Site

From 1959 through 1964, Pillar Point was an instrumentation site for the Navy's Pacific Missile Range.

In 1964, the Air Force made Pillar Point part of the Air Force Western Test Range.

Now, Pillar Point Air Force Station is the northernmost instrumentation site of the Western Space and Missile Center, located at Vandenberg Air Force Base. But no military personnel are stationed at Pillar Point. Instead, civilians who work for ITT Federal Services Corporation track missiles fired from Vandenberg and monitor space shuttles and satellites launched by NASA.

In the future, the huge dish antenna will track commercial space launches.

Today, it is hard to imagine how Pillar Point looked without its array of antennas and buildings. The first buildings went up during World War II, when Pillar Point was an observation post linking the Coastside to the Harbor Defenses of San Francisco. Underground bunkers built during the war still exist and are used for storage. After the war, the silhouette of Pillar Point changed even more. More buildings went up, along with missile tracking antennas.

Rockets were even fired from Pillar Point. In the fall of 1967, the Air Force planned to launch seven rockets, each bearing instrument-laden weather balloons. Fog cancelled a few of the launches. The remaining ones generated enough noise and burning exhaust gases to upset most Coastside residents. At each launching, a five-foot-long rocket blasted upward in a fireball from the muzzle of the launch cannon. Within 128 seconds, the rocket thrust itself to an altitude of forty miles, released its weather balloon, and then disintegrated. The weather balloon slowly descended, transmitting information on wind, temperature and air pressure.

Nowadays, there are no more rocket launchings. Instead, you can watch as the huge dish antenna rotates to track missiles fired from other places.

A few specifications: The crown of Pillar Point is 175 feet above sea level. The large dish antenna is 80 feet in diameter; its tower is 120 feet tall.

Pillar Point Ridge, Fitzgerald Marine Reserve and Seal Cove Fault

Narrow Pillar Point Ridge has two neighbors worth knowing. On the ocean side, Fitzgerald Marine Reserve protects the rocky tidepools. On the land side, San Gregorio fault (locally known as Seal Cove fault) menaces the Bay Area. This active fault comes ashore in Pillar Point Marsh, slashes along the base of the ridge, cuts through an old Native American campsite near Fitzgerald Marine Reserve in Moss Beach, and then reenters the ocean at Seal Cove. Geologists and archaeologists, after studying the Native American campsite, determined that the ocean side of the fault moves north a few millimeters a year. Any fault moving at that rate produces big earthquakes every 300 to 500 years. The last quake on San Gregorio fault was about 500 years ago.

Through the golden arch near Pillar Point Marsh pass some of the world's best surfers. In 1991, shortly after word of the monster Maverick's wave off Pillar Point leaked out, local surfers gave public notice that this wave was not for beginners. Pillar Point ridge is in the background.

Maverick's

To watch surfers challenge Maverick's, the biggest wave this side of Hawaii, go beyond the yellow gate and follow the trail to the ridge top behind Pillar Point. In the winter, offshore to the south, 50-foot waves hurl hardy surfers astride custom-made, big-wave boards 35 miles an hour toward Sail Rock. In the summer, surfers cruise along more moderate waves.

What makes Maverick's one of the world's biggest waves? Simple, the ocean floor and the winter storms. Just off Pillar Point, winter swells roll rapidly through a deep canyon until they hit a shallow reef. The water, with no place to go, roars straight up, making a terrifying Maverick's wave.

Only the best and the bravest surfers ride Maverick's.

Pillar Point Marsh Trail.

Pillar Point Marsh Trail

When you look at vibrant Pillar Point Marsh, you think that it must always have been cherished as a bird lover's paradise. Not so. In the 1970s, racing motorbikes, "hippy" busses, and dumped cars claimed this precious beach and marsh. Happily, San Mateo County now owns the marsh and has begun habitat restoration.

Bird watchers have tallied nearly one-fifth of all North American bird species in this tiny 35-acre Garden of Eden. Not too many such marshes—with a willow-choked fresh water creek at one end and a seaweed-encrusted salt water flat at the other—exist anymore. Year around, birds find Pillar Point Marsh irresistible for resting and feeding.

Garter Snakes

Many years ago, in early spring after a very wet winter, we watched scores of garter snakes sunning themselves on the tangle of half-submerged willow trunks in the marsh. We have never seen them since. Perhaps as the health of the marsh improves, more garter snakes will sun themselves in Pillar Point Marsh.

Some Birds at Pillar Point Marsh

About 650 bird species consider North America their home. With patience, you may spot over 100 of these species at Pillar Point Marsh. Take along a good bird book and binoculars for your outing. Maybe you will see these common birds, along with some of the others listed in this book.

☐ **Cinnamon Teal:** The male Cinnamon Teal is just that— cinnamon-red nearly all over. Look for these beautiful small ducks grazing on seeds and tender shoots near the edge of the marsh.

☐ **Mallard:** Whenever you think of a duck, you think of a Mallard. The male's shiny green head, white neck band, brownish chest and curled tail feathers are unmistakable, as is its very loud *quack.*

☐ **Snowy Egret:** If you spot a bird with snowy white plumage, a long neck, thin black bill, long black legs and yellow feet slowly stalking the shallows, check the box to the left.

☐ **Northern Phalarope:** In the winter, it is quite a sight to observe gray-backed, white-headed and white-chested Northern Phalaropes spinning in the marsh waters to stir up flies, larvae, water insects and tiny crustaceans to eat.

☐ **Barn Swallow:** Once we watched two fork-tailed Barn Swallows feed their four fledglings, who were precariously perched on the cable which cordons off the marsh from trespassers.

☐ **Common Yellowthroat Warbler:** In the spring, if you hear a *wichity-wichity* call from a shrub at the edge of the marsh, look for a small, black-masked warbler with a bright yellow throat and chest.

☐ **Yellow-rumped Warbler:** This slate-gray warbler with yellow throat, yellow rump and white wing bars is a frequent marsh visitor.

☐ **American Goldfinch:** Look for bright yellow American Goldfinches with black caps and black wings eating dried seed heads around the edge of the marsh. They often feed in flocks. Some folks call these birds "wild canaries."

Pillar Point Trail takes you to the west arm of the breakwater.

Pillar Point Trail

Pillar Point Trail leads you around two sides of diamond-shaped Pillar Point—first alongside the placid shore of Pillar Point Harbor and then alongside the rocky, surf-splashed reef of the open ocean. At the tip of Pillar Point, you can watch Maverick's wave heave against Sail Rock reef.

From the trail you get a good view of the eucalyptus forest surrounding El Granada. This forest, planted between 1906 and 1910 when the tract of Granada was new, has burned several times. During one of the fires, oldtimers took their children to safety on the beach, while in San Mateo (8 miles inland) people watched the smoke billow over the mountains.

Eucalyptus, once considered a fast-growing wonder tree, is now considered an ecological disaster. But no one knows what to do about eliminating it.

What would El Granada look like without its distinctive canopy of trees? Look a bit to the north to see more natural Coastside hills covered with grass and Coastal Scrub. Where would you prefer to live?

Montara Mountain, Pillar Point Marsh and the little point in the 1930s.

The Coastside and the Rest of the World

Until about 90 years ago, the Coastside was virtually isolated from the rest of the world. To the north, steep-walled Montara Mountain stymied early road builders trying to reach San Francisco. To the east, predecessors of Highway 92 tenaciously wound over a slight dip in the Santa Cruz Mountains to reach San Mateo. To the south, travellers dashed around Waddell Bluffs at low tide to reach Santa Cruz.

Out of desperation, Coastside farmers looked oceanward to get their potatoes, cabbages and red oats to San Francisco markets. In 1858, they built Denniston's Wharf, the first shipping wharf on Half Moon Bay. Denniston's Wharf extended from the little point in the center of the photo above. All traces of the wharf disappeared in 1959 when the U. S. Army Corps of Engineers leveled the point to build a road to reach the new breakwater site.

After 1868, farmers abandoned Denniston's Wharf, preferring to use Amesport Landing in present-day Miramar, which was closer to the growing town of Half Moon Bay. At low tide on winter days, you can still trace pilings of Amesport Landing. (See Walk 5.)

Romeo Pier, just east of Pillar Point Marsh, has always been a fish-receiving pier, never a farm-produce shipping pier. (See Walk 2.)

A Short Course in Coastal Scrub Plant Identification

As you walk Pillar Point Trail, take a few minutes to look at the 100-foot-high cliff alongside the path. On this easily overlooked rock face grow a good many Coastal Scrub plants which are also found on Montara Mountain, the mountain you see looming to the north. Coastal Scrub is the dominant native plant community on the Coastside.

White Flowers

Coast Buckwheat: Clusters of whitish-pink flower balls on top of foot-long stems mean only one plant: Coast Buckwheat. Dark green, wavy-edged leaves cluster around the base of the stems. May—October.

Coast Sagebrush: You will never forget Coast Sagebrush if you crush a few silvery-gray, thread-like leaves between your fingers. Tiny, whitish-yellow flowers appear from August through October.

Soap Plant: If you hike the trail in the late afternoon in May and June, you will certainly notice spidery-looking soap plant flowers. Hike in the morning and they won't be open. Native Americans used the fleshy root for soap.

17

Henderson's Angelica: Like white umbrellas on three-foot stems, Henderson's Angelica stands above all other flowers on this cliff. The umbrellas are made up of many tiny, very fragrant, white flowers. May—July.

Rattleweed / Locoweed: This trailside plant attracts everyone's attention, especially in the late summer, when the inch-long, bronze-colored, bladder-like seed pods appear. The whitish-green flowers are pea-like and on a stalk. June—August.

Coyote Bush: When you see a Coyote Bush, you know you are in Coastal Scrub. The female flowers (which look like tiny, fluffy shaving brushes) and the male flowers (which look like worn down shaving brushes) are on different plants. Coyote Bush is the most common shrub along the Coastside Trail. September—December.

California Blackberry: Thorny-vined, sprawling Blackberry has large white flowers with five petals. The berries, which appear in early summer, are at first red and very sour and then black and very sour. Leave them for the birds and small mammals. Look on page 86 to compare California Blackberry and Poison Oak. Never confuse them!

Pearly Everlasting: The papery white flowers of Pearly Everlasting linger nearly year round on Pillar Point. Its leaves have no fragrance. The leaves of a look-alike plant—Fragrant Everlasting—have a strong sage smell. Both are on Pillar Point.

Yarrow: Once you crush a feathery, dark-green yarrow leaf, you will never forget its pungent sage-like smell. Many small white flowers make up the flat-top cluster. April—October.

Yellow Flowers

Gum Plant: This low growing plant has many flowers with bright yellow petals. When the flower buds first form they look like saucers, full to the brim with sticky white gum. As the petals develop, the gum disappears. May—October.

Rosilla: Tall Rosilla has flowers with large brown domes which nearly obscure the tiny yellow petals underneath. Long narrow leaves form "wings" along the stems. May—July.

Lizard Tail: Shrubby Lizard Tail has dense umbrellas of tiny yellow flowers. The gray-green leaves are very fragrant. Lizard Tail, along with Coyote Bush and Coast Sagebrush, indicates Coastal Scrub. May—September.

Bluff Lettuce: This succulent has bright yellow, tube-like flowers. The greenish-red fleshy leaves are in a rosette at the base of the stem. May—September.

California Poppy: The cheerful orange of the most beloved California flower welcomes hikers along the trail. Sometimes you will see it in bloom year-round although peak flowering is in the spring. California Poppy is the state flower.

Field Mustard: Bright yellow field mustard, which came to California with the Spanish explorers, is in bloom nearly year-round. Many birds and mammals live off its tiny seeds.

Tree Lupine: Masses of shrubby Tree Lupines, with pale yellow, fragrant, pea-like flowers, give color to the cliff from spring through summer. The dark green leaves look like starbursts.

Beach Sagewort: Gray-green, velvety Beach Sagewort has no sage fragrance at all and you must look closely to see its tiny yellow flowers in the summer. It thrives in beach sand.

Bristly Ox Tongue: Aptly-named Bristly Ox Tongue is your constant companion for any hike along Half Moon Bay. It produces dandelion-like seeds by the thousands which grow wherever they land—on the sandy beach, in wetlands or on the rocky cliff. May—December.

Yellow Sand Verbena: Low-spreading Sand Verbena with its bright yellow, fragrant flowers and flat, fleshy, oval leaves colonizes shifting sands easily. May—October.

Red Flowers

California Bee Plant: Yes, square-stemmed California Bee Plant does attract bees to its tiny, tubular, dark red flowers. It towers over other plants, at three to five feet high. March—July.

Bull Thistle: Long yellow spines make this a dangerous plant even though the reddish-purple, powder-puff flowers are lovely. The plant can grow to four feet high. June—October.

Blue Flowers

Douglas Iris: A few colonies of lovely Douglas Iris greet walkers in the early spring. The colors range from pale to deep blue. After the flowers fade, the salty winds burn the grass-like leaves brown. Native Americans wove ropes from the fibers in the leaves. April—May.

Wild Radish: The white, pale blue or lavender flowers of Wild Radish are among the first (along with the yellow flowers of Field Mustard) to appear in the spring. Its fat seed pods have only two to ten seeds apiece, but many animals find them tasty.

Coast Aster: In the fall, long after most flowers are gone on the Coastside, the pale blue of many-petaled Coast Aster gives color to the brown trailside.

Horned Sea Rocket: Blue-flowered Horned Sea Rocket stabilizes the beach sand alongside the trail. The leaves are fleshy and the seed pods have two "horns" near the base. It is in flower nearly year-round.

Ferns

Wood Fern: Believe it or not, a few colonies of Wood Fern grow on this salty, windy cliff face. The leaflets of the triangular-shaped fronds are set in such a way that a wood fern looks like a partially closed venetian blind.

Bracken Fern: Bracken Fern grows on single stalks and looks like a very broad triangle. It dies back in the winter.

23

Harbor Birds

Pillar Point Harbor is a safe haven for hundreds of water and shore birds. Take along a bird book and binoculars and plan to spend at least an hour watching birds.

Once in the fall, on an offshore rock about the size of a three-car garage, we spotted these birds:

❑ Black Turnstones
❑ Caspian Terns
❑ Least Terns
❑ Cormorants
❑ Whimbrels
❑ Marbled Godwits
❑ Brown Pelicans
❑ Western Gulls

Other birds to look for include:

❑ Western Grebes
❑ Lesser Scaups
❑ Buffleheads
❑ Red-breasted Merganzers
❑ Loons

During the winter, flocks of Black Brant Geese graze on seaweed along the shore.

Abalone Farm

Farms in the harbor? Yes, indeed. Trapped in cages under the raft with blue floats at the end of the breakwater are thousands of baby Red Abalones. When first "planted" by the abalone farmer, they are about one-half inch long. Every week after planting, the farmer feeds them fresh kelp, and on this diet, within a year, they grow to two inches long. Then, it's off to Santa Cruz, where they put on another two inches, only to be sold as tasty delicacies in upscale restaurants.

You may find an iridescent shell from an uncaged Red Abalone when you beachcomb the sandy shore below Pillar Point.

Marine Mammals

Jagged Sail Rock attracts Steller's Sea Lions, Northern Elephant Seals, Harbor Seals and California Sea Lions. Most likely, you will see the bobbing head of either a curious California Sea Lion or Harbor Seal watching as you stroll the beach below Pillar Point. But how can you tell which one it is? Simple. Use your binoculars to see if the head has visible ears or not. A California Sea Lion has little external ear flaps. A Harbor Seal doesn't. Instead, it has tiny ear-holes hidden by fur.

Within the last few years, folks exploring the offshore reefs in kayaks report an increase in Sea Otters, everyone's favorite marine mammal.

Shells

At times, the sandy beach below Pillar Point seems paved with beautiful tiny shells and shell fragments. Look for these:

California Mussel   *Rock Oyster*

Volcano Limpet   *Turban Snail*

Beach Wrack

You are in the presence of beach wrack if you hear these comments: "Phew! It's stinky here!" "This beach is squashy!" "Look at all the flies!".

Beach wrack is kelp which has broken loose from the fertile reefs and washed ashore. Sometimes thousands of pounds of decaying kelp, along with thousands of dead marine animals that once lived in the kelp, lay rotting on the beach. Sandy-colored Beach Hoppers and low-flying Kelp Flies quickly colonize the decomposing wrack. Barn Swallows and Brewer's Blackbirds feast on the flies.

Walk 2

Pillar Point Harbor and Princeton–by–the–Sea

Distance: Pillar Point Harbor to Surfers Beach, three-quarters
mile. Princeton–by–the–Sea loop, one mile.
Parking: Free parking at Pillar Point Harbor and
at outer breakwater RV Park off Highway 1.
Beach access: Yes.
Picnic tables, bathrooms, drinking fountain: Pillar Point Harbor.
Wheelchair access: Pillar Point Harbor.
Note: The trail connecting Walk 2 and Walk 3 is not yet
completed. Use care if you walk along Highway One.

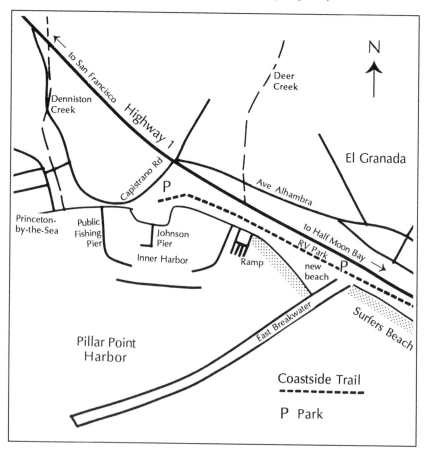

The masts of fishing boats dominate the views of Pillar Point Harbor.

Pillar Point Harbor: A Brief History and Some Trivia

For over 100 years, fishermen have sought safe anchorage for their boats below the headland of Pillar Point. But Pillar Point never offered refuge from the powerful winter storms out of the south. In 1911, after several fishing boats and their crews were lost during winter storms, Coastsiders agitated for a safe refuge. Many hoped that the U. S. Government would build a breakwater and fortify the harbor during World War I. In the 1930s, when the federal government was looking for projects to put people to work, Coastsiders went to Washington with plans for a harbor in hand. When it looked like war in 1939, they drew in a submarine and torpedo boat base.

After World War II, Coastsiders continued petitioning Washington for a safe refuge. In 1948, Congress designated Pillar Point as a harbor site to be developed by the San Mateo County Harbor District and the Army Corps of Engineers.

Nowadays, beached fishing boats are a rare sight.

In the 1950s, one plan for the proposed Pillar Point Harbor put a wharf in front of El Granada near the present-day Anchorage and Waves restaurants and ran a breakwater offshore near present-day El Granada Elementary School.

Work on the breakwater began in 1959 and was completed in 1961. Two serious problems were immediately apparent. First, the prevailing waves rounding Pillar Point, instead of gently striking Princeton's shores, bounced off the east breakwater and crashed upon the sandy beaches of El Granada and Miramar, quickly eroding the centuries-old shoreline. Second, winter storm waves out of the south surged through the harbor opening, tearing boats from their anchorages. In 1967, the Corps added a "rock arm" to the west breakwater, which helped the surge problem a bit. But a breakwater within a breakwater was needed. The inner breakwater, built in 1982, now provides safe anchorage during winter storms.

1991. The outer breakwater, the rock arm and inner breakwater of Pillar Point Harbor.

Harbor Trivia

The outer breakwater, installed between 1959 and 1961, was built from sandstone quarried at Davenport, forty-two miles south of Pillar Point. The boulders made the journey north on trucks. To get them to the end of the lengthening breakwater, engineers built a road on top of it.

The 1,050 foot "rock arm" extension to the west breakwater was added in 1967 to prevent wave surges in the harbor during winter storms. The greenstone and schist boulders came from a quarry in San Andreas, 155 miles away to the east of Stockton. They were transported by rail to Richmond, where they were loaded onto barges for the sea voyage south. In all, 200,000 tons of boulders were dropped from wave-tossed barges anchored off the west breakwater.

The inner breakwater, built in 1982 to further protect boats from being driven aground during winter storms, needed approximately 100 barge loads of stone and rubble transported from a Marin County quarry.

A Walk Around the Harbor

Johnson Pier: Begin your walk at Johnson Pier, the heart of the harbor. At the end of the pier, fishermen from the home ports of Montara, El Granada and Half Moon Bay unload their catch of the day. Who knows what you will see in huge crates, iced and ready to transport to Bay Area fish markets—crab, rock cod, squid, or salmon?

Local fishermen celebrate the ocean's harvest every year on Harbor Day, the last Saturday of September. They anchor their boats, man the barbecue grills, and serve up the tastiest of their catch.

Near the restrooms is the largest array of recycling bins you have ever seen. Pillar Point Harbor is the national model for successful marine debris recycling programs.

Public Fishing Pier: When you stroll toward Pillar Point from Johnson Pier, you find another pier to walk on—the public fishing pier built along one arm of the inner breakwater. Some of the best views of the harbor are yours from the end of this pier. About sunset, look inland to the Monterey Cypress trees, which shelter the Shore Bird Restaurant, to watch Black-crowned Night Herons leave their roosts for an evening of fishing in the harbor. Each one announces its departure with a raucous *quokk*.

Deer Creek and An Old Boat Launch Ramp: When you stroll south from Johnson Pier, you pass the other arm of the inner breakwater and the new six-lane boat launch ramp. At the launch ramp, pay homage to the remains of Deer Creek, which once ran free and lively over a waterfall at the base of the lone Monterey Cypress atop the bluff. Now it runs silently through a culvert under the approach to the launch ramp. Eighty years ago, crystal clear Deer Creek was the source of El Granada's drinking water.

Just below the two restaurants on the bluffs, stretching from the shore into the water, are the relics of pilings which contained a dirt-filled boat launch ramp built in the 1960s. The ramp, built by Ralph H. Rehbein, "The Hamburger King" and owner of the Sea View Drive-In (now the Anchorage Restaurant), lasted only a few years. The pilings are best seen at low tide in winter.

1991. The pilings of the boat launch ramp built in the 1960s. In the background, construction begins on the new six-lane boat launch ramp, which opened in 1992.

The New Beach: It is not often that you can watch a beach being born. Just inside the east breakwater is a beach that didn't exist before 1959. As construction on the breakwater progressed, the natural southerly flow of sand offshore was interrupted. Sand on its way to El Granada Beach and points south got hung up in the new harbor. As the expanse of sand grew, colonizing plants such as Ice Plant, Pampas Grass, Horned Sea Rocket and Yellow Sand Verbena took root. Shore birds—Great Blue Herons and Killdeer—found resting places near the high-tide puddles. Nowadays, the beach looks quite natural, as if designed by Mother Nature herself. Signs posted along the margins call it a natural habitat, which it has become.

Just beyond the breakwater, watch local surfers catch the waves. The trail continues south along the bluffs to Half Moon Bay and beyond.

A Fortune at Your Feet

Don't be fooled by mica masquerading as "fool's gold." A man and a woman once spent the better part of an afternoon picking up minute pieces of "gold" which glittered among the grains of sand on the new-born beach. The gold proved to be worthless, but the pleasant afternoon on the sunny shore wasn't.

The Princeton Inn, built in 1911 (ignore the 1906 date on the signboard), has seen plenty of good times and bad. The good times came first with the Ocean Shore Railroad and later with the rumrunners. The bad times have come recently: the Princeton Inn closed several years ago.

The Princeton Inn today.

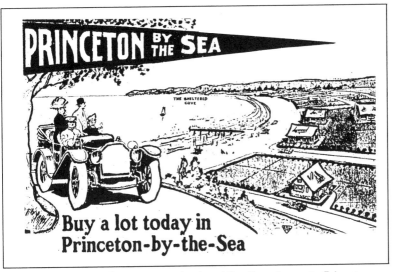

One of the many advertisements that lured San Franciscans to Princeton–by–the–Sea in the 1910s. (San Francisco Chronicle. June 16, 1911)

A Walk Around Princeton–by–the–Sea

When you stroll streets with grand names like Harvard, Stanford and Yale, you don't expect boatyards, small businesses, and pre-fab warehouses shoulder-to-shoulder with snug, eighty-year-old, hip-roofed bungalows. Yet, that's Princeton–by–the–Sea, a pipe-dream of a posh resort town from the days when the Ocean Shore Railroad (1908–1920) ran along the San Mateo County coast. Then San Franciscans frolicked on Princeton's sheltered beach, dined well at the Princeton Inn, and maybe bought a building lot or two along the well-sidewalked streets. During the Prohibition years (1920–1933), rumrunners, slipping in and out of the fog with Prohibition agents in pursuit, replaced the frolicking families.

Rumrunners and picnicking San Franciscans have come and gone, but Coastside fishermen have always remained loyal to Princeton. Before the turn of the century, this little fishing village was known as Denniston, named after the pioneer James Denniston, who built the first shipping wharf on Half Moon Bay. (See Walk 1.) Nowadays, many of the businesses you see serve local fishermen.

Begin your walk through Princeton at the large vacant lot across the street from the Shorebird Restaurant. A huge sardine cannery once processed thousands of pounds of fish here. Sardine boats unloaded their catch at a wharf attached to the round concrete structure just off the bluff. In the mid-1950s, the huge schools of sardines disappeared and the cannery closed. It was torn down in the early 1980s when a developer hoped to build a mini-mall on the lot.

Denniston Creek, a sad victim of the Coastside's need for water, sometimes flows alongside the vacant lot. Once abundant with Steelhead Trout, the creek was recently posted for containing unknown contaminants. Just before the turn of the century, some lucky prospectors panned a few pouches of gold from the sparkling waters of Denniston Creek. The Monterey Cypress trees lining the creek date from the days of the Ocean Shore Railroad.

To get a flavor of today's Princeton–by–the–Sea, continue your stroll along Princeton Avenue or Harvard Avenue. If the tide is out, you can return via the beach.

Romeo Pier

Romeo Pier is private property. Built over fifty years ago, this family-owned pier has supported several businesses—first a sardine cannery, then a fish fertilizer factory, and now a chemical fertilizer factory which meets the needs of commercial plant growers on the Coastside.

If you are diligent, you may spot a Belted Kingfisher perched on the wires above Romeo Pier.

Birds Along the Way

Pillar Point Harbor offers excellent bird watching. Take binoculars and a bird book. Each season brings its own birds.

In the Spring and Summer

Forster's Terns: A Forster's Tern will put you in mind of a "sea swallow," so graceful is its flight above the water. Then, spotting a fish below, it abruptly stops, folds its wings and plunges headfirst into the water. More often than not, it reappears with a shiny fish in its beak. It immediately takes flight, the fish flopping, with scavenging gulls in pursuit hoping for a free meal. Forster's Terns have deeply forked swallow tails, red feet and black-tipped red bills.

Caspian Terns: Every spring, raucous, *kwaak*-ing Caspian Terns and powerful winds out of the northwest arrive at our beaches about the same time. These large, gull-sized terns have heavy, orange-red beaks, black caps and shallow forked tails. From heights of fifty feet or more, with their heads and beaks pointing downward, they plunge after small fish. You can see Caspian Terns resting in small groups, their folded wings neatly extended beyond their tails, on the shore just inside the inner breakwater.

In the Fall and Winter

Willets: The arrival of two shorebirds heralds the coming of winter: Willets and Marbled Godwits. Grayish-white Willets with long straight beaks probe sand dampened by receding waves, searching for sand crabs. They take flight with a cry of *keleek-keleek* and a flash of black-white-black wing bands.

Marbled Godwits: These cinnamon-brown shorebirds with long, upward-curved beaks probe the damp sand at the water's edge for food. Willets and Godwits flock together on the shore.

Loons: Three kinds of loons visit Pillar Point Harbor in the winter: Arctic Loons (the most numerous), Common Loons and Red-throated Loons. They are hard to tell apart. Only Common Loons yodel, but rarely in the winter. Enjoy all three kinds of loons for their ability to dive, to stay underwater while you slowly count up to 100, and to resurface far from where you expect. Loons are solitary birds, riding low in the water with stubby necks and beaks held high. You will seldom see a loon on the shore. Its legs, set far back on its body, are perfect for powerful diving, but no good at balancing the bulky body on land.

Western Grebes: Western Grebes have very long white necks and slender yellow beaks. When sleeping, they curl their necks on their backs and look like plump tea kettles bobbing on the waves. Grebes can spend a long time under water searching for fish, which ornithologists think they spear with their pointed beaks! Look for large flocks or "rafts" of Grebes off Surfers Beach.

Red-Breasted Mergansers: Mergansers look wind-blown: they have shaggy crests of feathers extending from the backs of their heads. You will often see a male and female diving and fishing together. The male has a green head, white throat and reddish-brown chest. The female has a brown head.

Great Blue Herons: A solitary Great Blue Heron, standing four feet tall, often stalks the new beach, snatching up insects, mice and snails. If it takes flight, flapping wings which span seven feet, it may utter a rasping croak. Most likely, the herons that visit the harbor move on in the spring to Pescadero Marsh Natural Preserve to nest in the eucalyptus trees.

Year Around

Gulls: Gulls are confusing. The young go through color phases as they mature. Adult gulls of different species tend to look alike at first glance. Then, to add to the problem, the most common gulls in the San Francisco Bay Area—Western Gulls, Herring Gulls and Glaucous-winged Gulls—interbreed.

Look for Western Gulls with dark gray wings and Herring Gulls with black-tipped, light gray wings resting on the breakwater at dusk. Both have pink legs and yellow beaks with an orange dot at the tip. Or in the morning, enjoy watching them commute along the Coastside Trail to drink at Pilarcitos Creek. You may see them catching thermals over Frenchmans Creek subdivision on their way to the garbage dump on top of Ox Mountain. Late afternoon finds the gulls gliding along the bluffs, into the sunset, back to the breakwater.

Cormorants: To spot a Cormorant, look for a large black bird with head held high perched atop a boat mast. Or look along the breakwater until you spot a bird with wings spanning 50 inches stretched out to dry. Cormorants often fish in groups. They swim in a roughly shaped arc, diving and resurfacing more or less together. Brandt's Cormorants have bright blue throats in the spring.

Belted Kingfishers: It is a real treat to spot a Kingfisher atop a boat mast. At first you may take the still object for a mast ornament or a wind gauge, but suddenly a chattering Kingfisher, with an unmistakable crest of feathers on its head, flies up in a flash of blue. The Kingfisher hovers, then dives headlong into the water. Most likely it resurfaces with a fish in its thick black beak.

Killdeer: When startled, Killdeer fly low over shore and dunes, noisily *kree-kree*-ing. These distinctive birds have two black neckbands and white chests. Look for them just inside the breakwater on the new beach.

Walk 3

El Granada Beach

Distance: One-quarter mile.
Parking: Free parking at El Granada Beach parking lot. Street parking on Magellan Ave off Highway 1 in Miramar.
Beach access: Unimproved beach access from El Granada Beach parking lot. Cement steps to beach from Mirada Road at Magellan Ave.
Bathrooms and drinking fountain: No.
Wheelchair access: No.
Note: The Coastside Trail is not an official trail along the El Granada Beach bluffs (private property).

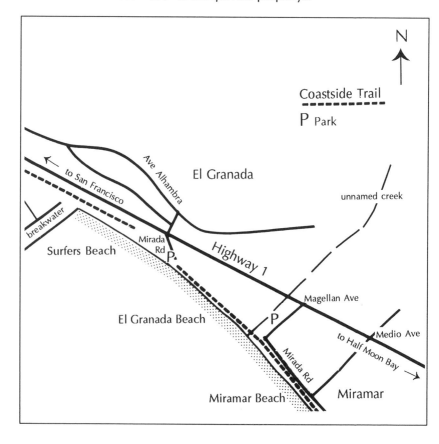

December, 1991. A bit of Mirada Road extends beyond the barricade at El Granada Beach parking lot. Before 1959, you could walk over 100 feet oceanward and still be on Mirada Road.

January, 1993. After just one year of heavy storms, the barricade on Mirada Road at El Granada Beach parking lot was dangling over the bluffs and more slabs of pavement lay on the beach below.

Here Today, Gone Tomorrow

The bluffs between El Granada Beach parking lot and Magellan Avenue in Miramar are the fastest eroding piece of shoreline in San Mateo County. At present, the official Coastside Trail has not been designated along the bluffs although it will be in the future. For now, walkers use the unimproved path and carefully stay away from the crumbling bluff edge. Notice how they keep beating out a new path as the old one falls into the ocean.

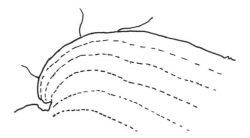

Pattern of prevailing waves out of the northwest in Half Moon Bay before the 1959 breakwater.

Bluff erosion started in 1959, when the Army Corps of Engineers installed the breakwater for the new Pillar Point Harbor. The much-needed and long-planned-for harbor was built to protect fishing boats from the southerly swells of winter storms. But from the beginning, it was obvious that the breakwater would drastically change the shoreline at Surfers Beach and southward. As the breakwater slowly extended into the ocean, the shore behind eroded more and more. Between 1959 and 1964, Surfers Beach lost an astounding twenty feet of shoreline per year. Today, the shoreline is still receding. Each year, on average, five feet of bluffs falls into the ocean between El Granada and Miramar.

How did this happen?

Before the breakwater was built, Pillar Point and Half Moon Bay formed a textbook example of a headland–bay coastline. For most of the year, the prevailing waves coming out of the northwest lost their energy bending around the headland of Pillar Point. They evenly struck the shore of Half Moon Bay from Princeton on southward. During the winter, the storm-driven waves out of the south dispersed their energy on the broad sandy beaches associated with a headland–bay coastline. Erosion was a constant three inches per year: the shoreline and the ocean were in near equilibrium. Coastside oldtimers remember those days: the beach in front of El Granada and Miramar, both winter and summer, was broad, sandy and safe.

After the breakwater was built, waves bending around Pillar Point literally ran into a stone wall. Their energy, no longer dispersed on Princeton's shores, smacked full-force onto the sandy beaches of El Granada and Miramar. The sand, built up over eons, could no longer protect the shore and soon fifteen-foot bluffs stood where once there had been broad beaches.

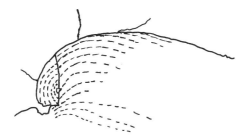

Pattern of prevailing waves out of the northwest in Half Moon Bay after the 1959 breakwater.

Today, the ocean is 150 feet closer to El Granada than it was in 1959. You can see the 150 feet for yourself on any winter's day at low tide. The ocean used to stop at the far line of partially buried riprap which runs parallel to the bluffs. In the late 1960s, San Mateo County installed the riprap to protect Mirada Road from the new wave pattern around Pillar Point. But Mother Nature was not to be denied. By 1971, most of the road was gone; the bluffs were still receding; and the riprap had dropped precisely where it had been installed, forever marking the ocean edge of Mirada Road. The slabs of pavement you see at the base of the bluffs are what is left of Mirada Road. Both slabs and bluffs are determinedly moving inland together.

Every winter, storms pound the base of the bluffs, sending spectacular plumes of water twenty to thirty feet into the air. Each crashing wave takes its toll. Soon the grave of "Bo Jay," marked by a small white cross just south of El Granada Beach parking lot, will fall into the ocean. Highway One at Surfers Beach barely manages to hold its own. This section of the Coastside Trail, when finally laid out, will always be threatened.

Who was Bo Jay? A beloved pet? Over the years someone has left shells and plastic flowers on the grave.

No one can predict when the breakwater, the ocean and the bluffs will find their equilibrium. After you witness some of the wildest winter storms, you may wonder if equilibrium will ever be achieved.

41

1991. Looking north toward the breakwater from El Granada Beach. The riprap on the left marks the edge of Mirada Road in the late 1960s. The slabs of pavement that once were Mirada Road lie at the base of the bluffs. The slabs move inland with the eroding bluffs.

1991. Looking south toward Miramar from El Granada Beach. El Granada Beach loses on average five feet of bluffs every year. The line of riprap on the right marks the 1960s edge of Mirada Road. One winter's day at low tide, pace off the distance between riprap and bluffs to measure the 150 feet lost to the ocean since 1959.

January 21, 1977. One of the last photos of Mirada Road.

Obituary for Mirada Road

Mirada Road between El Granada and Miramar died in the 1960s.

Mirada Road served Coastsiders well. In the 1850s, it was part of the county road between the town of Half Moon Bay and Denniston's Landing, a shipping wharf tucked below Pillar Point. Next it was part of the Coastside Boulevard, which was built in 1915 to show off the San Mateo County coast to San Francisco's Panama–Pacific Exposition visitors. Then, from 1938 through 1949, it was part of State Highway One. In 1949, when Highway One between El Granada and Miramar was rerouted inland to its present-day alignment, Mirada Road became a pleasant side road along the Pacific Ocean.

The cause of death was the building of the break-water at Pillar Point Harbor in 1959. The road's demise followed quickly as huge slabs of pavement fell into the ocean during winter storms over the next three years. In the late 1960s, San Mateo County tried to save the life of Mirada Road by dumping tons of riprap along its ocean side, but to no avail.

Viewing of the remains occurs every winter at the base of the receding bluffs in front of El Granada.

In 1910, the Granada bathhouse stood over one hundred feet offshore from the present-day shoreline at Surfers Beach at Highway One. Note the gentle beach.

1992. The badly eroded shoreline at Surfers Beach at Highway One. Compare the steep bluffs to the gentle beach in the photo above. In 1994, Caltrans installed more riprap and widened the segment of the Coastside Trail along the highway. Who knows how long this riprap will hold back the winter storms?

The steep beach access at El Granada Beach parking lot.

The first Ocean Shore Railroad passenger train from San Francisco to Granada in June of 1908.

"The future playground of the greatest good-time-loving people in the world." (1909 ad for Granada)

Piers, bathhouses, a casino, hotels, theaters, heated salt-water baths, promenades—a Coney Island on the Pacific Coast! In 1905, that is what the land company owning Granada wanted along this beachfront. So, Daniel H. Burnham, the famous landscape architect who designed the town, drew in a casino, two piers and some hotels on his town plan. But the land company had only enough money for one little bathhouse at present-day Surfers Beach. As it turned out, the greatest good-time-loving people in the world, the San Franciscans who rode the Ocean Shore Railroad to Granada, were perfectly content to enjoy the ocean and sand without the playgrounds. The Ocean Shore ran along the Coastside between San Francisco and Tunitas Creek, south of Half Moon Bay, from 1908 through 1920. When the railroad and the land company went out of business in 1920, a local farmer bought Granada's beachfront, which stretched from Miramar to Princeton, and planted it to artichokes. Until a few decades ago, the abandoned field that you see inland from the unimproved path along the bluffs grew some of the finest artichokes along the Coastside.

From the parking lot, you get a good view of El Granada and the Blue Gum Eucalyptus trees planted by the land company in the 1910s. The Ocean Shore Railroad track ran under the two blue buildings of the Wilkinson School in the foreground. It crossed present-day Highway One and the abandoned field to enter Miramar at Magellan Avenue. The roadbed dike is still visible at Magellan Avenue.

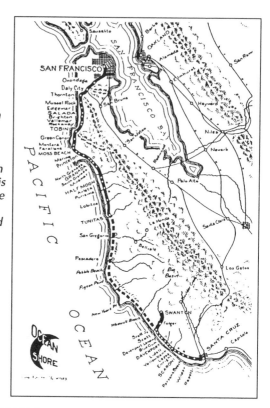

Route of the Ocean Shore Railroad, which ran along the San Mateo County coast between 1908 and 1920. Although not on the Coastside Trail, it is worth the detour to see the monument honoring Granada and the Ocean Shore Railroad which was erected by E Clampus Vitus, a men's history society, in September of 1994. The monument is at the corner of Plaza Alhambra and Ave Portola in downtown El Granada.

Adopt–A–Beach

El Granada Beach is the most heavily used beach on Half Moon Bay and—unfortunately—the most littered. Remains of illegal beach fires, leftover picnics, dirty diapers, abandoned blankets and beer bottles mar nearly every walk you take. The City of Half Moon Bay, which has jurisdiction over the beach, puts out trash cans, but they are often filled to the brim.

Hats off to the many folks who daily walk El Granada Beach, trash bag in hand, picking up after the inconsiderate.

El Granada Beach gets a good cleaning every September, when the California Coastal Commission sponsers its annual Coastal Cleanup Day.

---

*For more about the Ocean Shore Railroad, see Barbara VanderWerf's *Granada, A Synonym for Paradise: The Ocean Shore Railroad Years.*

A Candidate for a Vernal Pond

Just north of Magellan Avenue in Miramar is a candidate for a vernal pond. Near the grove of Monterey Cypresses is a small depression which fills with water only during the winter. A true vernal pond supports a unique assemblage of plants, generally annuals which flower in the spring. A true vernal pond is underlain by dense clay soil so that the water evaporates rather than drains. A true vernal pond has no shrubs or trees growing in it. In this case, the Monterey Cypresses growing at the pond's edge came after the pond. They were planted by neighbors living in Miramar. In aerial photographs taken between 1928 and 1946, the pond is treeless.

Vernal ponds matter. They are part of California's fragile system of wetlands. In fact, vernal ponds are found mostly in California, especially along the coastal terraces. Identifying a true vernal pond is a task for a biologist. Once a vernal pond has been identified, state and federal regulations protect it from destruction.

A few years ago, when this field was threatened by development, biologists began studying the pond as a potential vernal pond. Because the plan for development was withdrawn, the study was not completed.

In the winter, migrating shorebirds often rest near the pond and migrating hawks perch in the Monterey Cypresses. After the winter rains begin, the pond resonates with a chorus of Pacific Tree Frogs.

Sooty Shearwaters and Their Urge to Move

Nearly every year in the late summer and early fall, people jam the parking lot at El Granada Beach to watch in stunned amazement the low, swirling flocks of tens of thousands of Sooty Shearwaters. These birds, who circumnavigate the Pacific Ocean each year, generally show up right on schedule in late August. Some years they stay only a few days before their irresistible urge to move propels them onward. Other years—as in 1994—they stay for a month, if not longer. These silent, gull-like, dark-bodied and dark-winged birds feed on anchovies and crustaceans on the surface of the water.

Trying to count the birds is impossible. Just when you've begun to comprehend the vastness of one swirling flock at Surfers

Beach, you notice more swirling flocks off Miramar, Miramontes Point and Pillar Point. Some bird watchers estimate that millions of Sooty Shearwaters can swirl past the coast of San Mateo County on their way south.

Brown Pelicans

Brown Pelicans are never mistaken for any other water bird. Whether gliding in a long line following the crest of the waves or diving for anchovies, Brown Pelicans inspire awe in all coast lovers.

Brown Pelican watching is at its best during the summer and fall at El Granada Beach parking lot. A Brown Pelican looking for food is usually accompanied by a dark gray, red-beaked, raucous Heermann's Gull. The Pelican spots a fish, folds its wings and extends its neck. It dives, entering the water with beak shut. Instantly, its beak opens and its pouch encircles the fish. Water drains from the pouch as the Pelican's head surfaces. Now, as the Pelican sits on the surface of the water, it must toss its head back to adjust the fish in its pouch for swallowing. It is then that the Heermann's Gull hopes to steal the Pelican's fish. If you watch this act long enough, you will see that Heermann's Gulls are rarely successful.

Some Brown Pelicans linger through the winter, especially at Pillar Point Harbor where they become scavengers, accepting tidbits from fishermen. But most fly to breeding grounds along southern shores.

These magnificent birds, once nearly made extinct by the pesticide DDT in their food chain, appear along our shores in increasing numbers.

By-the-Wind-Sailors

In the spring, millions of By-the-Wind-Sailors, blown hither and yon at the whim of the winds on the open ocean, blow ashore on our beaches. Their cellophane-like sails atop the brilliant neon-blue bodies are canted perfectly to fly before the ocean winds. Each four-inch oval body is not a single creature, but a colony of specialists in all fields of survival—except that of navigation. Once ashore, the colony rots away, leaving only the sail behind to blow in the wind.

You always know when By-the-Wind-Sailors have beached, at first by the line of bright blue at the water's edge and then by the powerful reek of thousands of colonies rotting. By-the-Wind-Sailors are not dangerous: they do not sting.

Sand Dollars

El Granada Beach is the only beach along Half Moon Bay where you can find Sand Dollars—generally after the winter storms. What you pick up is actually a dead, bone-white Sand Dollar. Living Sand Dollars are covered with tiny, greenish-gray spines, which they use to get about in the shifting offshore sand. Topside, the beautiful five-pointed star indicates breathing tubes. Bottomside, the center hole indicates a mouth.

Winter storm at El Granada Beach parking lot, one of the best places for storm watching on the Coastside.

The Black Sand of El Granada

In the winter, black sand covers the shore below El Granada Beach parking lot. Actually, the "sand" is magnetite, an iron mineral which is strongly magnetic and very heavy. Take a spoonful home, let it dry out and then run a magnet through it.

Walk 4

Mirada Road in Miramar

Distance: One-quarter mile.
Parking: Street parking on Magellan Ave, Medio Ave and Mirada Road south of Medio Creek, all off Highway One. There is no street parking on Mirada Road along the ocean front. Medio Creek bridge on Mirada Road is a footpath only.
Beach access: Cement steps to beach from Mirada Road at Magellan Ave.
Bathrooms and drinking fountain: No.
Bench: Near Medio Creek bridge.
Wheelchair access: Yes, but use caution.
Note: This walk is along Mirada Road. There are no sidewalks.

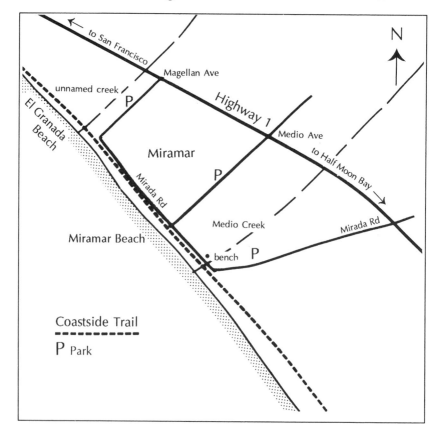

Two wind-shaped Monterey Cypresses stand on Mirada Road near the old bridge over the unnamed creek which flows out of El Granada. In the background is the Miramar Restaurant.

The bridge over Medio Creek was closed to automobile traffic in 1965. Now the bridge is only a narrow footpath.

A Tale of Two Bridges

This walk begins and ends with two washed-out bridges. Both bridges, built in 1915 as part of the magnificent Coastside Boulevard, which once connected Half Moon Bay to San Francisco, were sited a safe distance from the shoreline. Then, in 1959 when the Pillar Point Harbor breakwater was built, both bridges were doomed. The breakwater changed the wave patterns in

51

the bay of Half Moon Bay. The broad sandy beach along the shoreline between the two bridges immediately started eroding and fifteen-foot-high bluffs formed along the edge of Mirada Road, the old Coastside Boulevard. San Mateo County installed riprap which extended the life of this section of Mirada Road but didn't save the bridges. In 1965, both bridges were closed to automobiles.

The bridge to the north crosses an unnamed creek that comes out of the hills of El Granada. The bridge to the south crosses Medio Creek, which comes out of a canyon in Miramar. Both creeks flow only in the winter. The full name for Medio Creek is Arroyo del Rodeo de en Medio, The Creek of the Rodeo in the Middle. In the 1840s and 1850s, the creek was the boundary between two Mexican land grants. Every year, the two land grant owners held a rodeo in the canyon to sort out and slaughter their herds of longhorn cattle.

Nowadays, winter storms continue to nibble away at the two bridges and at the stretch of Mirada Road connecting them. The terrible El Niño storms of 1982–83 nearly finished them all off. But San Mateo County patched and filled the gaping roadbed and dumped more riprap. Notice the repair work as you walk along.

The riprap along Mirada Road makes beach access difficult.

In the 1930s, before the Pillar Point Harbor breakwater was built, the beach in front of the Miramar Restaurant sloped gently to the water's edge. At that time, Mirada Road was the main highway along the Coastside. On the ocean side of Mirada Road (the dark strip to the right), there was enough room for a parking lot. Note the small Monterey Cypresses in front of the house to the north of the restaurant.

1992. Mirada Road still runs in front of the Miramar Restaurant, but the parking lot and the gently sloping beach have disappeared. Instead, a fifteen-foot-high bluff mounded with riprap prohibits an easy stroll to the water's edge. In 1994, the seventy-year-old restaurant was remodelled to extend seating closer to the ocean.

The old Ocean Shore Railroad dike crosses Magellan Avenue near Highway One.

Reaches the Beaches

The Coastside Trail and the old right of way of the Ocean Shore Railroad have a lot in common. They cross the Coastside along nearly the same route between Magellan Avenue in Miramar and Kelly Avenue in Half Moon Bay. The Ocean Shore's slogan "Reaches the Beaches" enticed thousands of San Franciscans to journey south to buy lots in brand-new suburban tracts and to frolic on the Coastside's sandy beaches. Although Ocean Shore trains ran for only twelve years, between 1908 and 1920, they changed the look of the Coastside forever. Gone were the few scattered farm houses. Instead, nearly fifty suburban tracts, some with sidewalks and streets, sprang up along the railroad's line. Gone were the large grain fields. Instead, farmers grew artichokes, peas and Brussels sprouts. Today, tracts still line Highway One, the legacy of the Ocean Shore, and farmers still grow artichokes, peas and Brussels sprouts in the few remaining fields.

At Magellan Avenue, walk inland about four hundred feet until you come upon an obvious five-foot-high dike, which Magellan cuts through. Climb to the top of the dike and sight along it, both north and south. Eighty years ago you would have been standing in the middle of the Ocean Shore Railroad track. Just immediately around you, the suburban tracts of Shore Acres, South Balboa and Brophy's Beach, each only one or two blocks wide and stretching from the beach to the foothills inland, would have been staked out in twenty-five-foot lots which were to be sold to commuters and to vacationers. Not many houses were built in these three tracts.

Because the dike is plowed as a firebreak every July, its grass seeds sprout quickly in the winter rains, transforming the old Ocean Shore route between Magellan and Medio Avenues into a glowing green strip. The Ocean Shore track continued along the ocean side of Alameda Avenue to Medio Creek. There, a culvert to channel the creek was mounded with dirt to build up a roadbed for the Ocean Shore trains to cross.

Interesting Buildings and Old Trees

The aged, wind-shaped Monterey Cypresses and Monterey Pines along Mirada Road tell where the first buildings were. The two Monterey Cypresses in front of the house at Magellan Avenue and Mirada Road were once, in a different time with different values, studded with beer bottle caps.

During the Prohibition years between 1920 and 1933, rumrunners, flappers and bootleggers knew Mirada Road quite well. Today's Miramar Restaurant, then known as the Beach Inn Cafe, housed a speakeasy, complete with a bordello upstairs. On foggy nights, whiskey-laden ships from Canada hovered offshore along the three-mile limit, an invisible line protecting them from Federal Prohibition Agents. Sometimes Coastsiders sailed out to unload the whiskey ships, risking the chance of arrest by the "Pro-hi's" during the journey to shore. Other times, smugglers dumped their whiskey crates overboard for Coastsiders to retrieve along the sandy beach off Mirada Road.

The Bach Dancing and Dynamite Society really began with the music of Bach—and dynamite. Both literally exploded on the beach in 1964, the music from loudspeakers and the dynamite from the hands of drunken party-goers. Pete Douglas, connecting the two events, named his beach house and began a career of sponsoring concerts given by internationally known jazz and classical musicians. The original building, a tavern with a rough past, was quite tiny. Over the years, walls were knocked out, the first floor enlarged and a second story added to make the sprawling building you see today.

What looks like a huge sand castle with matching towers is actually an art gallery, which displays local artists. The Dunn Mehler Gallery opened in 1993.

Miramar Beach Health Club.

The Miramar Beach Health Club is visually stunning. Look for hidden faces in driftwood sculptures and a chimney with a human form. This is the headquarters of the Tsunami Rangers, a group of daredevil kayakers.

Enjoy the view of the ocean from the bench carved with the plea, "Love One Another."

Birds and Plants Along the Way

Surf Scoters: In the winter, you can watch Surf Scoters either ride the waves or dive through them just at the cresting point. "Scoters" is pronounced with a long *o*, as in *over*. The black males have heavy orange beaks and two white spots on their heads. Listen for the whistle of wings as Surf Scoters take flight.

Tree Mallows, riprap and Pillar Point.

Tree Mallows: Farmers once planted Tree Mallows in hedges around the vegetable fields which lined the San Mateo County coast. Tree Mallow, imported from Europe, withstands heavy winds and salt spray. It is a perennial and can grow ten feet high. Look for the lavender flowers in the spring and summer.

New Zealand Spinach: New Zealand Spinach, while not a true spinach, is nevertheless edible. Look for this low-growing plant with thick, fleshy leaves on top of the bridge over the unnamed creek and elsewhere along the Coastside Trail. The dark green leaves look like arrowheads. The small flowers grow at the base of the leaves next to the stem.

Walk 5

Medio Creek to Naples Creek

Distance: One-half mile.
Parking: Street parking on Mirada Road off Highway One. Fee parking at Roosevelt Beach via Young Ave off Highway One.
Beach access: At Alcatraz Ave and at Roosevelt Beach.
Bathrooms: Roosevelt Beach.
Water: No.
Benches: Near Mirada Road.
Wheelchair access: At Mirada Road and at Roosevelt Beach.

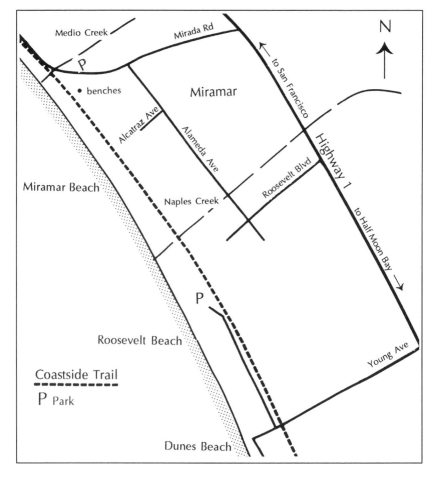

1910s. Miguel's Wharf in Miramar extended 1,000 feet into the ocean. Coastal steamers once tied up alongside to take on sacks of Coastside potatoes.

Miramar: The Wharf, The Town and The Hotel

On any winter's day at low tide, the pilings of an old wharf are exposed at Miramar Beach just south of Medio Creek. For about seventy years, from 1868 through the 1930s, the wharf served Coastsiders well. First known as Amesport Landing, the wharf was built by Josiah Ames to help solve the transportation problems of Coastside farmers. From 1868 through the early 1900s, coastal steamers pulled up alongside the wharf to take on sacks of grain and potatoes for San Francisco markets. When the Ocean Shore Railroad arrived on the Coastside in 1908, farmers sent out their produce by train. When the Coastside Boulevard was built over Montara Mountain in 1915, farmers sent out their produce by truck. The wharf soon fell into disrepair and by the 1930s was no longer considered safe.

The town of Miramar was quite a settlement in the 1910s, with hotels, a grocery store, warehouses, a soda drink factory, cafes and an elementary school—all to serve a population of 50, plus the many vacationers who arrived by train and auto. The Ocean Shore stop for Miramar was on the south side of Medio Creek.

In the 1920s, the Palace Miramar Hotel attracted hundreds of
daytrippers who enjoyed the gently sloping beach and Miguel's
Wharf (the new name for Amesport Landing). Medio Creek is to
the left of the hotel, out of the photo.

Miramar Beach, until 1959, had gentle dunes and a safe,
wide shore. Today, steep eroding bluffs prevent access to
the beach. Note that Miguel's Wharf was a working wharf
without guardrails. Promenaders needed to use caution.

The Palace Miramar Hotel

Opened New Year's Day, 1917.
Burned down September, 1967.

- Style of hotel: pavillion-bungalow
- Cost to build: $25,000
- Size of hotel: 70' by 300'
- 200' of glass windows facing the bay of
  Half Moon Bay
- 21 bedrooms, each with electric lights and call bells
- Dancing pavillion (50' by 70') with maple floor,
  stage, electric piano, concert grand piano
- Dining room (35' by 64') serving French, Italian and
  American food
- Barroom (13' by 24')
- Indoor salt-water plunge (25' by 70')
- Garage for guests arriving by auto

For many years, the Palace Miramar Hotel was the most imposing building on the Coastside. It opened in 1917 and boasted an indoor salt-water plunge and 200 feet of glass windows along its ocean front. Sometimes, to attract guests, Joe Miguel, the owner of the hotel, sponsored motorcycle races along the sandy beach, a beach use that seems strange to us today. During the Prohibition years, 1920–1933, rumrunners frequented the hotel and the wharf.

In the 1920s, motorcyclists revved up along Miramar Beach.

1992. The Coastside Trail, townhouses and an apartment building occupy the site of the Palace Miramar Hotel, which opened in 1917 and burned down in 1967.

The Palace Miramar Hotel stretched along the bluffs where the brown-shingled apartment building and townhouses are today. When the hotel burned down in 1967, a bit of Coastside lore went with it. The hotel might have been saved if the Pillar Point Harbor breakwater had not been built. The nearest fire hydrant was on the other side of Medio Creek, but the bridge had washed out in 1965. As the hotel burned, firefighters wasted precious minutes searching for another hydrant.

Be sure to note the old Monterey Cypresses planted along old property lines.

Monterey Cypress

Shoreline Erosion

The steep bluffs you see south of the Medio Creek bridge didn't exist forty-five years ago. Old photos show a sandy beach gently sloping to the water's edge in front of the Palace Miramar Hotel. The bluffs formed as the shoreline eroded after the breakwater at Pillar Point Harbor was built in 1959. The ocean quickly did its work. The bridge over Medio Creek was closed to traffic in 1965. The apartment building on the bluffs, built in 1972, had half its foundations exposed by 1984. By then, the parking lot north of the building had eroded to half its original size and the aged Monterey Cypresses along its edge were lying on the beach below. The bluffs are still visibly eroding. Note the washed-out beach access steps near the benches. The steps were built in 1991 and lasted until 1992.

The steep bluffs become natural dunes a bit further south, where the erosion is not so severe.

The steps to Miramar Beach, built in 1991, were washed out by 1992. In the winter at low tide, you can see the pilings of the old Miramar wharf just to the north of the steps. Compare the steep bluffs of today to the gently sloping beach of yesterday in the photos on page 60.

High Beaches, Low Beaches

Summer beaches are high. Winter beaches are low. That is why you can see the old riprap along eroded Mirada Road in front of El Granada and the pilings of the Miramar wharf in the winter, but not in the summer, when they are covered with sand.

In the winter, high-energy storm waves erode sandy beaches, carrying the sand out to deep-water sand bars. In the summer, smaller, calmer waves return the sand to the beach, building up dunes. If nothing interferes with this normal sand rhythm, a winter beach will have enough sand to protect it from winter storms. If a breakwater—such as the one at Pillar Point—has interfered with the natural buildup of sand along the shore, winter storm waves will sweep away the beach sand and the bluffs behind it.

Some day there may be an end to the erosion along Half Moon Bay. How would this happen? The sand eroded from the bluffs could replace the sand diverted by the breakwater. A wide beach could form to protect the bluffs and erosion could taper off. But no one knows when this would come about. In the meantime, building along the fragile, eroding bluffs is not a good idea.

Summer beach with high sand berm.

Winter beach with low sand berm.

The Rangers

At the intersection of Alcatraz Avenue and the Coastside Trail, walk gently through the front and backyards of the rangers and staff who care for Half Moon Bay State Beach. Although the houses are painted alike, their styles range from 1920s beach cottage to 1960s tract. For years, the peak-roofed house just a few feet inland from the trail used to be on the bluffs at Alcatraz Avenue. But the shoreline eroded and the house was moved inland in the 1970s.

Habitats Along the Way

Bluffs: A fine patch of ice plant grows between the apartment house on the bluffs and the rangers' compound. An import from South Africa, Ice Plant (more properly "Hottentot Fig") is now quite at home along California's shores, where it has been used to stabilize sand dunes. In the spring and summer, the yellow flowers emit a faint spicy smell. Its seeds are food for small rodents who in turn are food for the Kestrel you will most likely spot on the utility wires along Alcatraz Avenue. Kestrels hover while hunting the bluffs. Both males and females have black vertical neck stripes, a rusty back and streaked chests. The males have beautiful gray-blue wings. A Kestrel announces itself with a shrill *killy-killy-killy*.

Wetlands: The wetlands between Santa Rosa Avenue and San Pablo Avenue are rapidly disappearing as new houses are built. Soon to be gone are Pacific Tree Frogs, who after the first winter rains, fill Miramar with a chorus of song. Contrary to their name, these frogs are rarely found in trees. They are usually bright green with a black eye-stripe, but they can change their color to black within minutes.

One fine January day, after a week of heavy rains, I watched four families with small children listen in enchantment to the frog chorus. In the spring, you might see tadpoles in the drainage ditch alongside the trail.

The most common plant in the wetlands is the alien Bristly Ox Tongue. Note its yellow flowers and prickly, bumpy, linear leaves. Bristly Ox Tongue outcompetes everything, even Wild Radish and Field Mustard, which usually crowd out other plants.

For the past few springs, we have watched a nesting pair of Yellowthroat Warblers on the ocean-side of the trail. The bright yellow, black-masked male announces his presence with a *witchity-witchity* call from a twig of Bristly Ox Tongue.

You may also see a Song Sparrow, with its distinctive chest streaks ending in a center-of-the-chest spot. Once you learn his song, you will recognize Song Sparrows all along the trail.

Riparian Habitats: Naples Creek is lined with willows choked by German Ivy, identified by its shiny green leaves with pointed lobes. In the winter, German Ivy bears small, fragrant, yellow flowers. In the spring, aggressive Red-wing Blackbirds nest in the willows and dive-bomb walkers on the trail.

Look for the Anna's Hummingbird, its iridescent red throat flashing in the sun, which often perches on an inland willow. The male sings a squeaky song from his perch. Anna's Hummingbirds are on the Coastside year around.

Naples Creek is a good place to compare Milk Thistle and Bull Thistle:

A colony of Milk Thistle grows near the creek. In the spring and summer, the lightly spined leaves are blotched and lined with white—probably the reason for the name Milk Thistle. The large, red-purple, powder-puff flowers are very spiny. The stems have no spines. In the fall, the plant turns bronze.

Bull Thistle grows all along the trail. Its small, red-purple, powder-puff flowers are lightly spined, but its leaves have treacherous long spines as do the stems. It is in flower long after Milk Thistle.

You will see a Pumpkin Spider at Naples Creek in September and October. Guaranteed. Find a complicated web, gently tap a strong guy wire, and watch an orange, half-inch-long Pumpkin Spider come out to investigate. Sometimes you will find one resting upside-down in plain sight in the center of its web.

The S-curve through Naples Creek riparian habitat at Roosevelt Beach. Between Roosevelt Beach and Francis Beach, the Coastside Trail and the old Ocean Shore Railroad follow the same route.

Reaches The Beaches

When you walk the Coastside Trail between Santa Rosa Avenue in Miramar and Kelly Avenue in Half Moon Bay, you more or less follow the route of the Ocean Shore Railroad. One of the many tracts laid out along the line of the Ocean Shore was the City of Naples, which was two blocks wide and stretched from the shoreline inland to present-day Highway One. The City of Naples lies between Naples Creek, north of Roosevelt Boulevard, and an unnamed creek south of Washington Boulevard. On many maps, Roosevelt Beach is still called Naples Beach, a legacy of the days of the Ocean Shore Railroad.

Walk 6

Naples Creek to Frenchmans Creek

Distance: One-half mile.
Parking: Fee parking at Roosevelt Beach and at Dunes Beach via Young Ave off Highway One.
Beach access: Roosevelt Beach, Dunes Beach and Sweetwood Park (dry season only).
Bathrooms: Roosevelt Beach, Dunes Beach and Sweetwood Park.
Water: Sweetwood Park.
Benches and picnic tables: Sweetwood Park.
Wheelchair access: Roosevelt Beach and Dunes Beach.
Note: Only organized camping groups have access to Sweetwood Park by car.

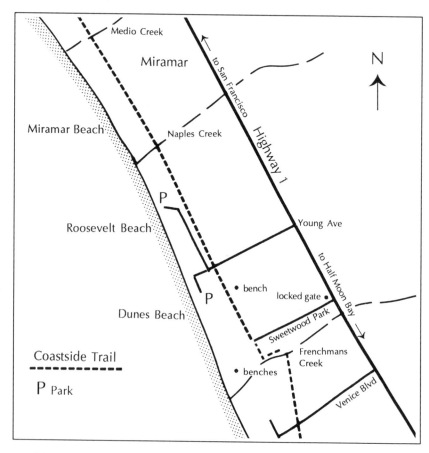

Ocean Shore Railroad trains once ran between the rows of Monterey Pines and Monterey Cypresses near the picnic tables in Sweetwood Park.

Reaches the Beaches

When you walk this stretch of the Coastside Trail, imagine what it was like in 1908 to ride along the same route in an Ocean Shore Railroad passenger car. Then, as now, the sand dunes blocked the view of the ocean, but the view of the inland hills was spectacular. Young Avenue, which leads to Dunes Beach and Roosevelt Beach, was supposed to be the main street of Surf Beach, one of the many suburban tracts laid out along the line of the Ocean Shore.

Near the picnic tables in Sweetwood Park, walk between the parallel rows of wind-shaped Monterey Cypresses and Monterey Pines. Ocean Shore trains going to and from San Francisco once puffed between the trees.

Sweetwood Park

On most weekends, colorful tents and active children fill the meadow at Sweetwood Park. The group camping site is part of Half Moon Bay State Beach.

Sweetwood Park was not always for group camping, and nearly everyone who walks through the park senses this. Surely, the Blue

69

Gum Eucalyptus, Monterey Cypresses and Monterey Pines were planted for some purpose, and the circular road laid out for a reason. Oldtimers remember ruins on the bluffs above Frenchmans Creek: house foundations and a red tile floor.

The story of Sweetwood Park begins with the Ocean Shore Railroad as do so many stories on the Coastside. Prior to the coming of the railroad, most of the Coastside, including the land we call Sweetwood Park, was planted to grain and potatoes. When Coastside farmers knew that the Ocean Shore Railroad was going to run along Half Moon Bay, they eagerly sold their fields to land speculators, who quickly staked out suburban tracts. By 1908 most of the frontage on Half Moon Bay had been subdivided into streets and building lots. Frank Martin, who owned the land on both sides of Frenchmans Creek, was a holdout. He let Ocean Shore trains run across his property, but he refused to subdivide. Most likely, he planted the parallel rows of cypresses and pines to screen the train as it puffed its way along the bluffs. Martin grew peas, fava beans and barley on his land until the late 1930s, when he tried to sell the beachfront to San Mateo County for a park. He wanted the park to be called Martin Beach, but the county was not interested. However, a Mr. and Mrs. Shuffleton from Oakland were. They bought the property north of Frenchmans Creek and transformed it into a vacation hideaway. Mr. Shuffleton, who had asthma, planted the eucalyptus grove near the highway in the hope that the powerful fragrance of eucalyptus would improve his breathing. The Shuffletons built a cabin on the bluffs near the mouth of Frenchmans Creek. Did the Shuffletons name Sweetwood Park? Most likely they did, in honor of the eucalyptus trees they planted.

In the late 1940s, after Mr. Shuffleton's death, Roger Duncan, who owned the horse stables south of Frenchmans Creek, bought Sweetwood Park. Duncan, in the business of rehabilitating injured race horses, built the circular road to exercise his patients.

In the early 1960s, Duncan sold Sweetwood Park to Dr. Westsmith, a San Mateo ophthalmologist, who used it for a weekend retreat until he rented it to Dr. George and Mrs. Cecelia Goldthorpe, well-known Coastside residents. The Goldthorpes enjoyed the blufftop house overlooking the ocean until 1967 when Sweetwood Park was purchased by the State of California for a park. The house on the bluffs, threatened by shoreline erosion, was torn down. But the foundations and red tile floor remained until just a few years ago, when the rangers dug them up to return the bluffs to natural habitat.

It is worth a detour off the Coastside Trail to stroll along the circular road where fine race horses once trotted through the eucalyptus grove which gave Sweetwood Park its name; to walk between the rows of trees which once screened Ocean Shore trains; and to sit on the benches above the mouth of Frenchmans Creek, where a vacation house once commanded an unbeatable ocean view. As you do so, note more traces of the various owners of Sweetwood Park: the row of coarse bamboo, planted as a wind screen along the north boundary; the wind-stunted acacias along the Coastside Trail; the spring-blooming narcissus and purple-blue periwinkles under the pines; the rambling roses along the circular road; and the sweet alyssum on the bluffs—all reminders of forgotten gardens.

Plants Along the Way

Coyote Bush: The presence of Coyote Bush means you are in Coastal Scrub. Coyote Bush covers our coastal hills, canyons and flatlands, thriving through our dry summers and wet winters. It comes in two varieties, both of which grow along the Coastside Trail. Close to the bluffs grows the dense, mat-like, prostrate variety, well adapted to harsh winds and salt spray. A few feet inland grows the upright, five-foot-high variety, which has many gnarled, woody trunks and a leafy umbrella of tiny toothed leaves. In bloom, both varieties produce small, white, fuzzy flowers which generate hundreds of windblown seeds. In wildfires, Coyote Bush explodes into flame, but it regrows quickly from charred trunks. Some folks call the shrub Coyote *Brush*, as opposed to Coyote *Bush*.

Look upon a Coyote Bush as an apartment building: some birds perch on the crown, the top story; some birds nest and feed in the middle story; and some birds, along with rabbits, feed on the ground floor, under the lower branches.

Tree Lupine: Four-foot-high Tree Lupines grow near the ranger kiosk at Dunes Beach. In the spring and summer, they bear lovely stalks of yellow pea-like flowers. In the fall, the long seed pods dry up and twist to scatter seeds. The leaves look like starbursts, with five or more leaflets radiating out from the center.

Poison Hemlock and Wild Fennel: There are two plants along the Coastside Trail which you must never confuse. Seen side by side, they are obviously quite different. But the problem begins when they are seen separately. Both plants are tall—five feet or more. Both plants have umbrella-like flower clusters. Both plants grow in the same area. But there is a difference: Poison Hemlock is deadly poisonous; Wild Fennel is edible, its leaves and seeds taste like licorice. Make sure that you can tell them apart before you experiment. Or, better yet, do not experiment. A good place to compare and contrast Poison Hemlock and Wild Fennel is at the ranger kiosk for Dunes Beach. Just north of the kiosk is a patch of Wild Fennel. Just south of the kiosk is a large patch of Poison Hemlock.

Here is a handy chart:

Poison Hemlock	Wild Fennel
• **Deadly poisonous**	• **Edible**
• Five feet plus tall	• Five feet plus tall
• White flowers in umbrella-like clusters; summer	• Yellow flowers in umbrella-like clusters; fall
• Parsley-like leaves	• Feathery, thread-like leaves
• Cat spray smell	• Licorice smell
• Purple blotches on stalks	• Blue-green stalks
• Single stalks	• Stalks in clumps

Coast Aster: In the fall, when most wildflowers are no longer in bloom, the pale blue of Coast Asters stands out from the brown of dried grasses along the trail. The plants are about two feet tall; the blue petals on the flower heads radiate from yellow centers.

Wild Radish   *Field Mustard*

Wild Radish and Field Mustard: No one can miss Wild Radish and Field Mustard along the Coastside Trail. Both grow right up to the very edges of the trail. Wild Radish has four-petaled, whitish-blue-to-blue flowers and long thick seed pods. Field Mustard has four-petaled, bright yellow flowers and long thin seed pods. In the spring, the fields along the trail are vibrant with their colors.

California Poppy: Golden orange California Poppies are in bloom nearly year around along the Coastside Trail. In the spring, look for a magnificent display near the entrance to Roosevelt Beach. When the temperature drops and on foggy days, the four-petaled flowers fold up tightly. California Poppy became the state flower in 1903. You may spot a poppy which doesn't look quite like a California Poppy. It is a near relative—low growing with small leaves and yellow petals with red centers—and is called Beach Poppy.

Yarrow: Fragrant Yarrow, with its sage-like smell, grows right to the edge of the trail. Look for a plant with dark green, fern-like leaves and a white, umbrella flower head on top of a one-to-two-foot stalk.

Fragrant Everlasting: Look for the gray-green leaves and white papery flowers of this fragrant one-to-two-foot-tall plant which grows nearly year around along the trail.

73

Mugwort: A tall dense colony of Mugwort grows near Frenchmans Creek bridge. Its gray-green leaves are shaped like goose feet and they smell like sage. The tiny yellowish flowers are in inconspicuous spikes at the top of the stems. Mugwort is very common and once you know it, you see it everywhere.

Fireweed: After the Coastside Trail was finished, park rangers spread seed-ladened hydro-mulch along its edges. Fireweed was the most vigorous survivor. It has tiny red-purple flowers on two-foot stems. In the fall, the long narrow seed pods peel back to release hundreds of seeds on parachutes. Soon we will be seeing a lot more Fireweed along the trail.

Coast Madia: Tall and sticky—that's Coast Madia. Its tiny yellow flowers are in inconspicuous nodding clumps at the top of four-foot stems. One touch of this plant leaves your fingers quite sticky.

Wild Oats: The Spaniards brought Wild Oats to California in the 1790s, along with their longhorn cattle. Gracefully drooping panicles of Wild Oats turn Coastside hills and fields golden brown by late spring. Wild Oats indicate rich soils.

Foxtail Barley: All dog owners know about Foxtail Barley, which produces bristly seed heads that find their way into the eyes, ears and noses of their pets. Watch out for this spiky grass along the trail. The dried seed heads will penetrate your socks and pants.

Birds Along the Way

White-crowned Sparrows: These busy birds perch year around on top of the Coyote Bush along the trail and feed on seeds on the ground below. Adults have black and white stripes on their heads, brown backs, and gray throats and chests. Listen for their distinctive song in the spring and the summer. Coastside White-crowns sing a slightly different song from that of San Francisco White-crowns, an observation that fascinates ornithologists.

House Finches: Gregarious House Finches are common in the Coyote Bush nearly year around. The males have rosy red to yellow heads, chests and tail spots. These thick-beaked seed-eaters sing joyously in the spring and summer.

Ravens: The raven population on the Coastside is booming. Ten years ago, it was an event to see a pair fly overhead. Now, groups of ten or more are common. Look for Ravens perched on the top of the bluffs along the trail, at the mouth of Frenchmans Creek, and in the Monterey Cypresses above the picnic tables in Sweetwood Park. Listen for their distinctive *kruach*. These huge, black, heavy-beaked birds mate for life. If you see one, look for a second. Often, they dine on dead sea birds on the beach.

Meadowlarks: What a treat to spot a Meadowlark perched on top of a Coyote Bush, its glowing yellow chest crossed by a black V-shaped bib. Meadowlarks tend to group together and, when startled, take off in low flight, showing their white-bordered stubby tails. Listen for their flutelike trill in the spring.

Mammals Along the Way

Brush Rabbits: Sometimes you will see a Brush Rabbit nibbling grasses at the edge of the trail. But most times you will only sense a scurry of brown fur out of the corner of your eye as a Brush Rabbit takes shelter under a Coyote Bush. These short-eared cottontails are about a foot long and feed on grasses and roots.

Jack Rabbits: Occasionally you will be startled to see a Jack Rabbit bounding through the Coastal Scrub at a rapid speed. If you follow its course, you may see it stop and freeze, its seven-inch-long ears on the alert for a pursuer. Jack Rabbits feed on grasses, roots—and most likely the nearby farmers' crops.

Gophers: Not even the Coastside Trail is immune to Gophers. In places, they have managed to break through the firm trail surface. Mostly, however, they dig tunnels along the edges of the trail, indicated by the mounds of freshly dug dirt. If you spot a Gopher, chances are you will see just its brown head with long yellow incisor teeth poking above a newly dug mound. Gophers are vegetarians with enormous appetites.

Trees Imported by Man

Blue Gum Eucalyptus, Monterey Cypress, Monterey Pine—these three trees dominate the Coastside landscape. Yet not one is native to the Coastside. During the time of the Native American Costanos, the Coastside was treeless, except for willows and Red Alders along the creeks. When Europeans settled here in the early 1800s, they brought with them a need for trees. At first, they planted Monterey Cypress and Monterey Pine, which were native to the Monterey area. Next, they planted Blue Gum Eucalyptus, which was imported from Australia to the Bay Area in 1853.

Monterey Cypress: Look for rugged Monterey Cypresses in Sweetwood Park. Planted as windbreaks, they have done their work well: there is no mistaking the prevailing wind direction along these bluffs. Monterey Cypresses have small, scale-like leaves which are closely set on cord-like branches. The cones, covered with what look like small shields, are one to two inches across.

For millions of people, the picture-postcard view of a wind-shaped Monterey Cypress atop an ocean bluff means "California." But Monterey Cypress grows only in a very small section of coastal California, from the Monterey Peninsula north through the San Francisco Peninsula.

Monterey Pine: Monterey Pines are very fast growers. For proof, keep your eye on a seedling along the trail for the next few years. Monterey Pines have four-inch needles in bundles of threes. The five-inch lopsided cones stay on the tree in clusters for a long time. It takes heat—either from a fire or a very hot day—for the cones to open and release their seeds. On a day when the temperature rises over 90 degrees, stand in Sweetwood Park and listen to the seeds pop from the Monterey Pine cones.

Blue Gum Eucalyptus: Some folks cannot imagine coastal California without Blue Gum Eucalyptus. The trees seem so at home, growing quickly and reseeding themselves easily. Yet all kinds of eucalyptus, including Blue Gum, were imported from Australia in the 1850s, some brought in as potential lumber trees, others as garden ornamentals.

On the Coastside, you are never out of sight of a Blue Gum—its distinctive silhouette dominates every view. The Blue Gums in Sweetwood Park are about sixty years old; those in El Granada are over eighty years old. The sickle-shaped leaves are about seven inches long. The whitish flowers turn into blue-gray seed capsules, one inch wide. Enjoy their pungent smell at all times, but most especially when it is raining.

Walk 7

Frenchmans Creek to Pilarcitos Creek

Distance: One-half mile.
Parking: Fee parking at Venice Beach via Venice Blvd off
　　　Highway One.
Beach access: Venice Beach.
Bathrooms and drinking fountains: Venice Beach.
Wheelchair access: Venice Beach.
Note: Horseback riders have the right of way over Frenchmans
　　　Creek bridge.

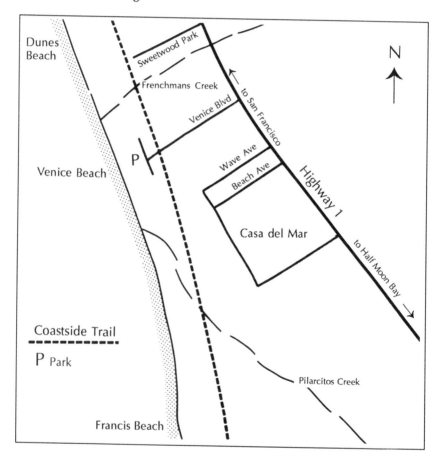

Ocean Shore Railroad trains ran just behind the ranger's house at Venice Beach. Perhaps this was someone's dream home—an ocean view out the front window and transportation at the back door.

Reaches the Beaches

The engineers who built the roadbed of the Ocean Shore Railroad knew about winter storms on the Coastside—about how storm runoff could transform placid creeks into swirling torrents within a few hours. Yet, they routed Ocean Shore trains across Frenchmans Creek on an earth-mounded culvert and across Pilarcitos Creek on a low pile bridge. Washouts occurred frequently, causing costly delays for passengers and freight.

During a winter storm, stand on the bank of either of the two creeks and watch the water swirl past. Our normal rainfall of about twenty-one inches a year can send both creeks raging into the ocean. Unfortunately for the success of the Ocean Shore Railroad, the early years of its operation were exceptionally wet ones. In 1909, thirty-two inches of rain fell; in 1911, thirty-one inches; in 1914, thirty inches. In just one month, January of 1911, sixteen and one-half inches of rain fell, washing out track all along the line. On a stormy night in 1911, would you have crossed a pile bridge over swollen and raging Pilarcitos Creek in an Ocean Shore train to reach your suburban home in the tract of Arleta Park in Half Moon Bay?

Along the line of the Ocean Shore between the two creeks, real estate speculators laid out three suburban tracts: Venice, El Mar Beach and Ocean Spray. Lots sold quickly but most likely the house in the photo above was the only one built. Today, three streets from those tracts survive: Venice Boulevard leading to Venice Beach, and Wave Avenue and Beach Avenue in the subdivision of Casa del Mar.

Notice the beautiful clean sand at the mouth of Pilarcitos Creek. Here, the Ocean Shore ran a spur line out onto the beach for the EB & AL Stone Company, which mined some of the Coastside's finest sand for use in San Francisco.

The Coastside Trail and the Ocean Shore Railroad follow more or less the same route in this section.

Names

Legend has it that the first "Frenchmen" to visit what we call Frenchmans Creek were Canadian horse thieves who stopped by in the 1840s. By the 1860s, their remembered visit had named the area Frenchmans Field. By the late 1870s, it was Frenchmans Gulch. And by the 1890s, our name of Frenchmans Creek had taken hold permanently. Note that Frenchmans is singular and has no 's.

Pilarcitos Creek has had two names. The Spanish explorers, led by Gaspar de Portolá, christened it Arroyo de San Simon y San Judas when, in October of 1769, they camped near the mouth of the creek on their trek north from San Diego. Portolá and his men were worn out. They had been marching for over three months and they hoped to meet a supply ship in Monterey Bay. By the time they reached Pilarcitos Creek, they suspected that they had missed Monterey Bay but decided to continue onward. In a few days, they became the first Europeans to see the expanse of San Francisco Bay from present-day Sweeney Ridge in Pacifica. Sixty years later, Mexican land grant owners renamed the creek Arroyo de los Pilarcitos, creek of the little pillars, after the distant headland of Pillar Point.

Inland Views Along the Way

Rising above the marine terrace which we call the Coastside is a northwest-southeast range of hills capped by three peaks: North Peak on Montara Mountain at 1,898 feet, Scarper Peak at 1,944 feet, and Sierra Morena at 2,315 feet. Montara Mountain rears over the forested hills of El Granada; Scarper Peak is due inland; and Sierra Morena (Brown Mountain) looms above Skyline Boulevard to the south. Of the three, Montara Mountain is not forested. Scarper Peak used to be *Scarpa Peak,* after its former owner, George Scarpa, an Italian immigrant who came to San Francisco in the mid-1850s. Coastsiders converted *Scarpa* to *Scarper* after the turn of the century.

Montara Mountain   *Scarper Peak*   *Sierra Morena*

The bridge over Frenchmans Creek opened in 1990. To cross the swollen creek during the winter months before then, walkers had to go inland to use an abandoned highway bridge adjacent to Highway One.

The bridge over Pilarcitos Creek opened in 1994. Don't be alarmed if it sways as you cross: the bridge was built to the highest earthquake standards. Also, the metal surface is rusty on purpose—to protect it from salt spray. The plaque honors John Hernandez, the Half Moon Bay resident who spearheaded the Coastside Trail project.

Riparian Habitats Along the Way

Frenchmans Creek and Pilarcitos Creek offer different close-up views of riparian habitats. Enjoy a bird's eye view from the bridge across Frenchmans Creek. Enjoy a frog's eye view from the bridge across Pilarcitos Creek. In the winter, note that both creeks flow north below the bluffs for some distance before entering the ocean. During the rainless summers and autumns both creeks are usually dry.

Pilarcitos Creek will often form a lagoon between the trail and the dunes at Venice Beach. The lagoon provides drinking water for hundreds of sea gulls and shorebirds, and the dunes a resting place. You can see huge flocks of birds nearly year around. A few paths lead from the trail for a closer view. In the fall of 1992, a dam burst on private property upstream and layers of silt smothered all plant and animal life in Pilarcitos Creek and the lagoon. It may take years before the creek and lagoon are once more viable ecosystems.

Both riparian habitats are dense with plant and bird life. Look for the following plants. Some are more obvious in one habitat than the other.

Willows: Several kinds of willows grow along the creeks, providing nesting places for many birds, including Red-winged Blackbirds, Mourning Doves and Hummingbirds. Look for abandoned nests in the winter when the willows shed their leaves. In the summer, look for the red galls on the long, narrow leaves which indicate nurseries for gall wasp eggs. In January, look for "pussy willows," a sure sign of spring.

Red Alder: Downstream from Frenchmans Creek bridge grow a few Red Alders. In the winter, identify them by their clusters of dangling brown, cone-like fruits and yellowish-green catkin tassels. In the summer, identify them by their four-inch, coarsely-toothed leaves. Red Alders are only found along streams entering the ocean in the narrow coastal strip between Santa Barbara and British Columbia.

Hedge Nettle: No need to fear Hedge Nettle, for it is not a true nettle and will not sting. Rub a stiff, hairy leaf and then smell your fingers. Not a very pleasant smell. Square-stemmed Hedge Nettles, about two feet high, bear a single stalk of purplish-blue, lipped flowers in the spring and summer. Stinging Nettles, also along the trail, have obvious bristly hairs on the stems and coarse leaves: leave them alone.

California Bee Plant: "California Bee Plant" sounds much more attractive than this plant's other name: Figwort. Yes, the nectar dripping from the plant's small, dark red flowers does attract bees and hummingbirds. A Bee Plant grows from three to five feet high and has large, triangular, dark green leaves. Gently feel its dark red stem: isn't that the squarest stem you have ever felt?

Cinquefoil: Look for low-growing Cinquefoil in the damp soil along Pilarcitos Creek. Its leaves are made up of from six to thirty toothed leaflets, and its five-petaled flowers are bright yellow.

Cattail: Everyone knows cattails. Look for them in Pilarcitos Creek. Native Americans ate the roots and young shoots, and wove mats from the older leaves. In spring, Red-winged Blackbirds stake out nesting territories from the tops of cattails.

Watercress: In the winter, the mouths of both Frenchmans Creek and Pilarcitos Creek are choked with a carpet of Watercress. Pungent-tasting watercress is protected: do not gather it. In the spring, watch flocks of bright yellow, black-capped American Goldfinches harvest watercress seeds produced from tiny white flowers. During the dry summer and fall, the watercress disappears, only to grow back with the coming of the winter rains.

German Ivy: German Ivy is ubiquitous in riparian habitats along the Coastside Trail. This invasive sprawling vine, with its year around bright green, pointed leaves and winter-blooming, fragrant yellow flowers, chokes the native vegetation along both Frenchmans Creek and Pilarcitos Creek.

Horsetail: Like stacked tubes, each segment of a horsetail fits neatly into the next. In the spring, a brown cone tops the tubes, producing reproductive spores. In the summer, each tube sprouts long green stems—the horse's tail. You can feel the grainy silicon in the tubes, which oldtimers used to scour their dirty dishes.

Hooker's Evening Primrose: Growing on a stout stem in damp places and alongside the trail is a three–foot tall beauty. From early summer through late fall, the large, yellow, four-petaled flowers demand your admiration. Get to know Hooker's Evening Primrose along the trail and you will see it flash by as you drive along Highway One.

Monkey Flower: In the drainage ditch just north of Pilarcitos Creek bridge grow a few Monkey Flowers. At the top of a single stout stem bloom bright yellow "monkey faces" with red dots. Two petals stand up straight; three petals stick out horizontally like a pouting lip. Leaves are somewhat fan-shaped with radiating veins. Look for Monkey Flowers during the summer.

Four Stinging Plants

Spend some time on Pilarcitos Creek bridge to get to know these four stinging plants, which threaten to overgrow it:

- ❑ Stinging Nettle
- ❑ Bristly Ox Tongue
- ❑ Bull Thistle
- ❑ California Blackberry

Trailside Plants

Beach Sagewort: Velvety, gray-green leaves distinguish Beach Sagewort. Certainly its tiny yellow flowers and non-sage smell don't. The leafy stems grow about two feet tall and the plant thrives in beach sand.

Beach Bur: Happily growing in mats in the sand near Pilarcitos Creek bridge is a small colony of Beach Bur. The little yellow flowers, which become spiny burs, look like upside-down pillows hanging in clusters from long stalks. Leaves are silvery green.

Beach Primrose: All along the trail—generally near a protecting fence post—grow yellow-flowered, prostrate Beach Primroses. The one-inch flowers have four petals; the leaves are light green. You will find cheerful Beach Primrose in flower nearly year around.

Lizard Tail: Clumps of tiny mustard-colored flowers on top of deeply cut, dark-green, sage-smelling leaves make this classic Coastal Scrub shrub easy to identify. Look for it near Pilarcitos Creek bridge. Why the name Lizard Tail? Maybe it's the lizard-like leaves.

Poison Oak and California Blackberry: Yes, there is Poison Oak along the Coastside Trail. Pause above Frenchmans Creek in Sweetwood Park, just oceanward from the bathrooms. Here, three plants grow intertwined: Poison Oak, California Blackberry and German Ivy. Identifying German Ivy poses no problem. Use this handy chart to tell California Blackberry from Poison Oak:

Poison Oak	California Blackberry
• No thorns on stems or leaves	• Thorns on stems and leaves
• "Leaves of three," meaning each leaf has three lobes	• "Leaves of three," meaning each leaf has three lobes
• Shiny green leaves turn red in fall	• Dull green leaves turn red in fall
• Loses leaves in winter	• Keeps leaves in winter
• Small white flowers	• Large, five-petaled white flowers
• Bunches of small, shiny, smooth white berries	• Black, hairy, edible "real berry-looking" berries
• Grows as a bush and as a climbing vine	• Grows as a sprawling vine

Birds Along the Way

Northern Harriers: If you see a hawk with a broad white band across the top of its tail, gliding a few feet above the ground, long wings held in a slight "V" and tilting from side to side, you have spotted a Northern Harrier searching for rodents. Female Harriers are brown; males are gray. Some folks still use the old name of "Marsh Hawk" for these lovely birds.

Red-tailed Hawks: You will almost certainly see a
Red-tailed Hawk on your walk along the Coastside
Trail. Look for a Red-tail perched on a utility pole
along Venice Boulevard leading to Venice Beach.
The Red-tail may slowly drop from its perch upon
its prey—a snake, mouse, or gopher. Or it may
spiral in an updraft to soar above the field. Or, if
the wind is stiff enough, it may hover above the
field watching for prey. A Red-tail has several color
phases, but the russet-red color of the top surface
of its tail always confirms its identity, as does its
four-foot wing span.

Red-shafted Flickers: In the winter, you will most
likely hear a Red-shafted Flicker before you see it
as it gives out its *flick, flick* call from the top of a
Coyote Bush. In flight, an eleven-inch-long Flicker
shows wings that are red underneath, a white
rump band, and a black bib across its white chest,
which is spotted with black. Flickers cling to the
sides of tree trunks and power poles, using their
powerful beaks to dig out insects.

Mourning Doves: Look for gray Mourning Doves
perched on the utility wires along Venice
Boulevard and feeding in flocks on the ground in
the horse pastures south of Frenchmans Creek.
The wings of Mourning Doves whistle when they
take flight. Their mournful *coo-coo* is heard along
the trail in the spring and summer.

Brown Towhees: Towhees make a *tenk, tenk*
sound while scratching for insects and seeds
beneath the Coyote Bush. These robin-sized birds
are beautifully brown with a reddish-orange patch
under the tail.

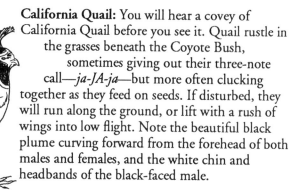

California Quail: You will hear a covey of California Quail before you see it. Quail rustle in the grasses beneath the Coyote Bush, sometimes giving out their three-note call—*ja-JA-ja*—but more often clucking together as they feed on seeds. If disturbed, they will run along the ground, or lift with a rush of wings into low flight. Note the beautiful black plume curving forward from the forehead of both males and females, and the white chin and headbands of the black-faced male.

Black Phoebes: Black Phoebes are solitary. If you spot one, it will most likely be perched on the tip of a dead stalk, flicking its tail while it waits to fly off to nip an insect in mid-air. Often it returns to the same perch. Black Phoebes have black heads, backs and chests, and white bellies. Their heads look squarish in profile. Listen for the plaintive call, *ti-wee, ti-wee.*

Bush Tits: Listen for the communal wheeze of high, thin notes as these busy, tiny, long-tailed birds move in flocks through trees and along the tops of the Coyote Bush looking for insects. Acrobatic Bush Tits can dangle upside-down from twigs and leaves.

Red-winged Blackbirds: In the spring, from Pilarcitos Creek bridge, you can watch male Red-wings atop willow bushes sway in the breezes and give out raucous calls that sound like *kon-kree.* They space themselves evenly in the willows, each male needing about fifteen feet of elbow room all around. Luckily, no one need intrude in their territory: Red-wings are famous for dive-bombing trespassers.

Two former vegetable fields viewed from the Coastside Trail just south of the ranger kiosk at Venice Boulevard. Farmers recently abandoned the field on the left: Coyote Bush is just beginning to take over. Farmers abandoned the field on the right long ago: it is dense with Coyote Bush. Notice the Pampas Grass in the field on the right. Eventually it will spread to the field on the left.

From Grasslands to Artichokes to Coastal Scrub

When the exploring Spaniards walked across the Coastside marine terrace in 1769, they noted native bunch grasses, Coyote Bush and a few willows along the creeks. There were no forests on the Coastside then. For thousands of years, Native Americans had used what grew on the marine terrace—grass seeds and cattails for food, and willow branches for shelter frames. The Spanish and Mexican cattle ranchers following the explorers introduced some of the plants familiar to us today. Within a few years, their Wild Oats, Foxtail, Wild Radish and Field Mustard choked out the native grasses. By the 1860s, American farmers and ranchers had cleared much of the Coastside, including the hillsides, for crops of oats, wheat, hay and potatoes. After the Ocean Shore Railroad arrived on the Coastside in 1908, the flatland fields were planted to artichokes, peas, Brussels sprouts and other vegetables; the hillside fields remained planted to grain and hay.

Today along the Coastside Trail, the communities of Miramar and Casa del Mar occupy some of the old vegetable fields. The rest of the fields, abandoned years ago, are in different stages of becoming Coastal Scrub.

Once farmers decide to "let their fields go," that is, not plant artichokes or Brussels sprouts any more, the first plant colonizers to take over their fields are fast-growing annuals which produce thousands of seeds. These annuals—Wild Radish, Field Mustard, Wild Oats—build up the soil for the slower growing woody perennials which follow—Coyote Bush, Poison Oak, California Blackberry and Tree Lupine. The annuals and woody perennials, joined by Yarrow, California Bee Plant, Pearly Everlasting, Poison Hemlock and Wild Fennel, make up the Coastal Scrub we see along the Coastside Trail.

If you stand on the Coastside Trail just a bit south of the ranger kiosk at Venice Beach and look inland, you will see a sharp line dividing two abandoned fields. The field toward the ranger kiosk was abandoned about fifteen years ago. Only a few Coyote Bush stand out among the grasses, Wild Radish and Field Mustard. The field toward the community of Casa del Mar was abandoned a long time ago. It is nearly filled with Coyote Bush and is a good example of Coastal Scrub. Someday, the field with just a few Coyote Bush will look like its neighbor, and walkers on the Coastside Trail will see one continuous sweep of Coastal Scrub between Venice Boulevard and Casa del Mar.

Coastal Scrub is dense: only rabbits, mice, snakes and small birds can penetrate it. It takes our intense, salt-laden winds well. It survives drought and fire. Coastal Scrub is tough, but it may not survive Pampas Grass.

"Sort-of" Brussels Sprouts

Look along the ocean edge of the Venice Beach parking lot for reminders of when these fields grew vegetables. Growing along the bluffs are "sort-of" Brussels sprouts plants, "sort-of" broccoli plants and "sort-of" cabbage plants which have all gone wild out of cultivation. Once upon a time, the old fields inland helped feed San Francisco.

Coyote Bush vs. Pampas Grass

Coyote Bush belongs here. Pampas Grass doesn't. Both are excellent colonizers. Both can grow quickly in disturbed soil. Unfortunately, Pampas Grass grows a little more quickly. If someone carves a road across Coastal Scrub, chances are it will be lined with full-grown Pampas Grass before Coyote Bush has a chance to get started.

White fluffy Coyote Bush flowers grow on tiny stalks; white fluffy Pampas Grass flowers grow on beautiful plume-like stalks. Guess which flower stalk gets picked and carried about by walkers along the Coastside. Guess which of the two plants humans help spread.

If Pampas Grass gets started, it is almost impossible to get rid of. Ask the Half Moon Bay State Beach rangers who have used back-hoes to route it out. Leave the tiniest bit of root in the ground and next year, you have another Pampas Grass plant to dig out.

Why should anyone want to get rid of Pampas Grass? Simple. Pampas Grass outcompetes native shrubs, including Coyote Bush. Coyote Bush provides food and shelter for Coastside birds and mammals. Pampas Grass, with its razor sharp leaves, shelters and feeds no one.

Where did Pampas Grass come from? The Bolivian Andes. Who imported it and when? Growers in the 1950s imported Pampas Grass to use for erosion control along coastal California highways. Did Pampas Grass take to our climate? Did it ever! By the 1960s, it had spread over the entire California coastal zone. Some ecologists think it could eventually replace most native plants, including Coyote Bush. What will the Brush Rabbits, the California Quail and the White-crowned Sparrows do then?

Along the Coastside Trail, the worst growth of Pampas Grass is adjacent to Venice Boulevard.

Pampas Grass

Coyote Bush

Walk 8

Pilarcitos Creek to Kelly Avenue (Half Moon Bay)

Distance: One-half mile.
Parking: Fee parking at Francis Beach via Kelly Ave off
Highway One.
Beach access: Francis Beach.
Bathrooms and drinking fountains: Francis Beach.
Picnic tables and camping: Francis Beach.
Wheelchair access: Francis Beach.
Note: Half Moon Bay State Beach Headquarters is at
Francis Beach. Take Kelly Ave to reach downtown
Half Moon Bay, one mile inland.

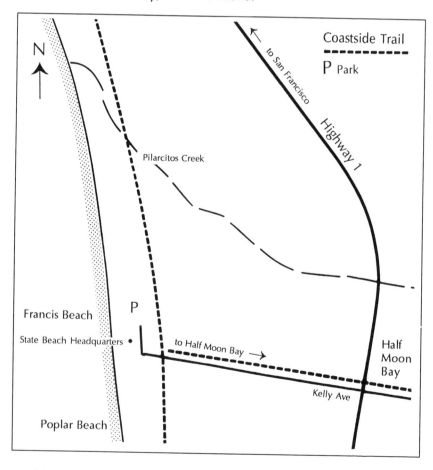

A bicycling family sets off on the Coastside Trail at Francis Beach.

Reaches the Beaches

Francis Beach was once a desirable suburban tract on the line of the Ocean Shore Railroad. Now campers in RVs and tents enjoy ocean-side living (albeit temporary) where eighty years ago San Franciscans planned to build artistic bungalows.

The Coastside Trail in this section is divided by a chain link fence: horseback riders use the inland trail, and walkers and bike riders use the oceanward trail. Between Pilarcitos Creek and the bend in the fence near the ranger's kiosk, the horse trail is exactly on the old Ocean Shore Railroad roadbed. At the bend, sight south along the diagonal fence line to where you see a row of houses facing open space. Those houses front the route of the Ocean Shore.

The Half Moon Bay depot sat near where the track crossed Kelly Avenue. In 1930, the depot was dragged one mile inland to the Community United Methodist Church on the corner of Johnston and Miramontes Streets to become its social hall. You can see it there today.

Why did the Ocean Shore Railroad bypass the town of Half Moon Bay when the route was laid out in 1905? At that time, Half Moon Bay was a thriving agricultural center in need of better transportation to get farm produce to San Francisco markets. Farmers, who depended upon the winding mountain road to San Mateo and on coastal steamers at Amesport Landing in present-day

Miramar (see Walk 5), welcomed the coming of the railroad. The railroad surveyors were more than willing to run the track down the middle of Main Street. But in August of 1905, the townspeople voiced strong objections to a train through their town. Consequently, the surveyors sited the track—and the Half Moon Bay Station—one mile oceanward. After all, the Ocean Shore's slogan was "Reaches the Beaches."

A marine terrace

The Marine Terrace We Call Home

If you live on the Coastside, you probably live on the marine terrace. If you drive Highway One, you drive on the marine terrace. If you walk the Coastside Trail, you walk on the marine terrace.

The Coastside as a marine terrace is the stage for the story of our lives. From the ocean bluffs to the base of the first hills, from Pillar Point to Miramontes Point, stretches fairly flat land which once was ocean floor. During the Ice Ages, shifting earth movements raised the ocean floor at the same time that the sea level was fluctuating. The sea level went down when the climate turned cold. Water froze into glaciers and the ocean was far away from the present shoreline. Fifteen thousand years ago, you could walk on a broad plain to the Farallon Islands. The sea level rose when the climate turned warm. Water melted from the glaciers and waves cut into the broad plains, creating marine terraces. Waves still cut into our Coastside marine terrace as the sea level continues to rise. Before the Pillar Point Harbor breakwater was built in 1959, the waves cut on average three inches of shoreline per year. After the breakwater was built, the shoreline in places has lost from five to six feet per year. Our marine terrace is diminishing real estate.

The Four Seasons

Winter

On a winter day, watch the storm clouds pile up over the ocean and Miramontes Point. The southerly winds can be quite brisk and have been clocked at ninety miles an hour at the Pillar Point Tracking Station. Storm-driven waves smash against the base of the bluffs in front of El Granada and wash over the breakwater, flooding the harbor beach. You may see gray sheets of rain over the ocean as clouds dump their loads before reaching land. The rain, when it comes, will be at your back as you walk toward Pillar Point. As the storm abates, the wind turns and the rain comes from the northwest.

You can predict the onset and departure of a storm by watching chimney smoke or by watching how raindrops hit the windows of your house. When a storm approaches the Coastside, raindrops will strike your south-facing windows and blow your chimney smoke to the northwest. When a storm leaves the Coastside, raindrops will strike your northwest windows and chimney smoke will drift to the south.

In a normal year from November through March, the Coastside will get about twenty-one inches of rain. In a wet year, look for thirty inches or more. In a dry year, we squeak by with about fifteen inches.

Note the creeks along the Coastside Trail, both named and unnamed. Unnamed creeks, some no more than drainage ditches, begin trickling with the first heavy rains. Named creeks, usually dry in the fall, turn into torrents, carrying downstream debris which has clogged the creek since the last cleansing winter storms. Some wet years, Frenchmans Creek and Pilarcitos Creek continue to flow into the ocean well into the summer. From the trail along Francis Beach, look inland into Frenchmans Creek Canyon below Scarper Peak. This watershed funnels enormous quantities of runoff into the narrow creekbed at Sweetwood Park.

After one month of rain, the hills and fields green up. New shoots of Field Mustard, Wild Radish and Yarrow line the trail. By March, many plants will be in bloom.

Walking on the trail in a winter storm is exhilarating. Use extreme caution crossing the flowing creeks and walking along the slippery bluffs.

The Largest Animal Ever

On the lawn of Half Moon Bay State Beach Headquarters is the skull of a Blue Whale, the largest of all animals ever to exist. If you pace between the skull and the white stake 100 feet away, you begin to comprehend how large is large. A Blue Whale weighs 160 tons and eats eight tons of krill—one-fifth its body weight—every day!

Spring

On a spring day, you can walk from Pillar Point Harbor to Kelly Avenue with a fine breeze at your back. But when you turn around for the return walk, you discover that the fine breeze has grown into a driving, breath-stealing gale. The Coastside is notorious for its spring winds out of the northwest. The morning breeze may start out gentle enough, but by afternoon the wind is howling along the shoreline and the driving beach sand covers up all the morning's footprints.

The spring winds bend and shape the Monterey Cypresses and Monterey Pines along the trail. Notice how they all lean towards the southeast, showing lush green growth on the lee side and spiky twigs on the windward side.

In the spring, flowers carpet Coastside fields in a riot of yellow, orange, white, blue, pink and red. But the winds quickly dry out the grasses. By April, the Wild Oats are golden brown.

Snowy Plovers

From April through August each year, the dunes along Pilarcitos Creek lagoon are closed to beachgoers. Inside the fence, female Snowy Plovers find small depressions in the sand—perhaps an old footprint—to lay three tiny, off-white, speckled eggs. If the parents are lucky—and no people or dogs trample their eggs, nor ravens or sea gulls maraud the nest—after twenty-eight days, three more Snowy Plovers will be added to the state's dwindling population. In 1989, only 1,386 Snowy Plovers were counted in California. In 1991, two Snowy Plovers tried to raise a family on these dunes, but Ravens got to the nest before the eggs hatched.

This stretch of dunes is one of the few remaining Snowy Plover nesting sites in the state. Please help give Snowy Plovers a safe and quiet place to raise their young.

Summer

On a summer day, you can start your walk at Pillar Point Harbor in the fog, enjoy sun along the trail in front of El Granada (known by residents as "sunny El Granada") and be back in the fog at Frenchmans Creek. Summer means fog to Coastsiders. Most days, morning fog burns off by afternoon, receding to the Great Fog Bank which rolls south offshore along the coast. Then by early evening, the temperature drops a few degrees and the fog rolls onshore. There are periods when the sun never breaks through the fog. August is the worst month. Some fog watchers have counted 29 days in a row in which Coastsiders never saw the sun.

Fog can blanket the Coastside Trail quickly. Once, on a rare hot summer day, the beach in front of El Granada was packed with people seeking relief. Warm air, apparently saturated with moisture, blew across the waves and sunbathers. Then something happened to drop the temperature of the water a few degrees: the tide may have turned, or a cool ocean current may have drifted past. Quickly, small wisps of fog formed over the waves as the cooling air released its moisture. The wisps joined, creating an instant fog bank over El Granada Beach. Hundreds of beachgoers hastily packed up and within minutes were in their cars on Highway One, which turned into a parking lot as traffic came to a standstill. The fog from the shore blew across the highway; people turned on their headlights and windshield wipers as they slowly edged homeward in a Coastside traffic jam.

Stand in Sweetwood Park on a foggy day in the dry, rainless Coastside summer and enjoy the sound of dripping water and the smell of eucalyptus. Notice how fog drips off the eucalyptus leaves, which were perfectly designed to capture and direct air moisture to the root systems. Some botanists estimate that a eucalyptus forest can "catch" an extra ten inches of moisture a year. The vegetation below the eucalyptus in Sweetwood Park remains fairly lush year around while the rest of the Coastside is dry and brown, no matter how much fog blows over it.

The summer fog makes the Coastside cool enough for crops of artichokes, peas and Brussels sprouts. Note the farmers' fields inland from Francis Beach.

Fall

On a fall day, the weather on the Coastside Trail will be just right: no fog, no harsh wind, a gentle sun. The Coastside's real summer comes in September and October. But by the end of October, Coastsiders are waiting for the first rains of November. The vegetation along the trail and in the hills is tinder-dry. Everyone dreads the land winds out of the east, those hot, dry, unsettling winds which can stir a spark into a holocaust in minutes. Fortunately, the winds from the east are infrequent and the rains soon arrive to end fire danger on the Coastside.

In the fall, the creeks are nearly always dry. Along the trail, the blue of Coast Asters stands out among the dried-out, brown plants. The rains will soon be here.

Buildings Along the Way

In 1983, about where the Coastside Trail crosses Pilarcitos Creek, the Sewer Authority Mid-Coast (SAM) built a great sewer outfall line into the ocean for disposal of wastes treated at its plant just inland.

The administrative building for Half Moon Bay State Beach, which is made up of Francis Beach, Venice Beach, Dunes Beach, Roosevelt Beach and Sweetwood Park, is at Francis Beach. The building used to be a blufftop restaurant called the Moon Dream Cafe.

Where the Coastside Trail crosses Kelly Ave is an old shed and loading platform, both relics of the days when artichokes grew as far as the eye could see. In 1920, after the Ocean Shore Railroad stopped running, farmers loaded their artichokes onto trucks which backed up to this platform. The diagonal fence line indicates the route of the Ocean Shore.

Turn inland at Kelly Avenue to explore downtown Half Moon Bay, one mile away.

COASTSIDE TRAIL

A COOPERATIVE EFFORT BY:
CITY OF HALF MOON BAY
STATE OF CALIFORNIA
DEPARTMENT OF PARKS AND RECREATION
COASTSIDERS FOR SAFE BIKEWAYS

SIGNIFICANT FUNDING SOURCES:
STATE COASTAL CONSERVANCY
METROPOLITAN TRANSPORTATION COMMISSION

DEDICATED: OCTOBER 4, 1992

Plaque marking the Coastside Trail at Francis Beach.

Walk 9

Poplar County Beach to Miramontes Point

Distance: Three-quarters mile from Kelly Ave to Poplar County Beach parking lot via the bluffs. Three-quarters mile from Poplar County Beach parking lot to Miramontes Point via the beach.

Parking: Fee parking at Francis Beach via Kelly Ave off Highway One. Free parking at Poplar County Beach via Poplar Street off Highway One, and at Miramontes Point via Redondo Beach Road off Highway One.

Beach access: At Poplar County Beach and at Francis Beach. Beach access at Miramontes Point is extremely difficult and dangerous.

Horses: Poplar County Beach.

Bathrooms and water: No.

Wheelchair access: Yes.

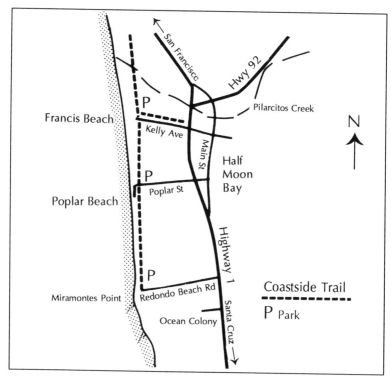

In 1946, twenty-six years after the last Ocean Shore train left for San Francisco, the Arleta Park depot looked derelict. In 1990, the depot (at the the corner of Poplar Street and Railroad Avenue) was restored as a private home.

Reaches the Beaches

South from Kelly Avenue, the Ocean Shore Railroad and the Coastside Trail part ways: the trail clings to the bluffs; the route of the railroad swings inland, paralleling Highway One to the end of the line at Tunitas Creek.

The yellow Arleta Park depot, now a private home, is at the corner of Railroad Avenue and Poplar Street, about one-quarter mile inland from Poplar County Beach parking lot. The tract of Arleta Park, with "large twenty-five-foot lots, graded streets, alleys through every block, shade trees in every lot and water piped in every street," was laid out in 1906, two years before the first Ocean Shore trains from San Francisco pulled into the station. Promoters touted Arleta Park as "the favorite suburban residence site for San Francisco." At $225 per lot, nothing down and $2.00 per week, most lots sold quickly. But few houses were built.

As you walk the trail along the bluffs, look across the grassy field and imagine Ocean Shore trains puffing their way to Arleta Park station. For twelve years, from 1908 through 1920, the shrill whistle of locomotives rolled out to sea across these bluffs.

The U. S. S. De Long, a navy destroyer, ran aground on Poplar Beach in December of 1921. It was refloated.

Who knows what interesting relics you will find on Poplar Beach?

During a terrible storm in March of 1898, the three-masted, iron-hulled New York ran aground below Kelly Avenue in Half Moon Bay. Note Pillar Point in the distance. (San Francisco Call Bulletin. March 15, 1898)

The Shifting Sands

In March of 1983, just after a fierce El Niño storm, a Montara resident took a stroll along the beach south of Kelly Avenue. There on the sand was a wooden boom with hand-forged rope pulleys. A few days later, a Half Moon Bay resident discovered what seemed to be metal hull plates from an old ship. By the time State Beach rangers investigated, the relics had been buried by the shifting sands.

The ghost of the sailing vessel *New York* once again had run aground on Poplar Beach. Eighty-five years earlier, a similar March storm drove the iron-hulled sailing vessel, bound from Hong Kong to San Francisco, ashore. Fortunately, there was no loss of life—just the cargo and the ship itself. When the ship beached at the foot of Kelly Avenue, the whole town turned out to aid in rescue and salvage operations. The *New York* slowly broke up in the surf—and bits and pieces still wash ashore.

Along the bluff tops just south of Kelly Ave, concrete rings and piers remind us of World War II on the San Mateo County coast.

World War II Relics

No, the three concentric concrete rings along the bluff tops had nothing to do with the gangster Al Capone and Coastside rumrunners during the wide-open Prohibition years (1920–1933) —even though oldtimers like to wink and tell that story. But fact still blends with local lore when the real story is told. During World War II, the Navy operated a gun fire school on this site. Naval gunners, firing small guns mounted to the concrete rings, aimed at offshore targets. Oldtimers—with a wink—claim that Sail Rock off Pillar Point to the north was much bigger before World War II than after.

After every rainy season, some of the concrete piers tumble closer to the beach. Seeping ground water, which erodes the bluffs, is the culprit—not the Pillar Point Harbor breakwater.

Monterey Bay National Marine Sanctuary

In September of 1992, all the coastline for as far as you can see and beyond, from the Farallon Islands to San Simeon, became federally protected waters. Covering 360 miles of California coast (5,312 acres) the sanctuary is larger than Yosemite National Park. Hundreds of species of birds, fish, marine mammals and plants are now protected forever.

A Walk along the Bluffs

Native Coastal Scrub is slowly colonizing the old grain fields inland from the trail. This is a good place to compare the two kinds of Coyote Bush. Dwarf Coyote Bush grows in ground-hugging mats close to the edge of the bluffs, while its larger relative, Coyote Bush, grows in patches inland. Non-native Bristly Ox Tongue, one of the most common plants along the Coastside Trail, dominates the bluffs. It is an opportunist, rapidly moving into recently abandoned fields, eventually to be replaced by native Coastal Scrub. In the winter, the dandelion-like seeds feed many birds, especially bright yellow American Goldfinches.

A few timid colonies of native plants, including Sea Pink and Lizard Tail, cling to the degraded bluff tops.

Sea Pink

As of this writing, the residents of Half Moon Bay debate the future of this magnificent open space. For now, enjoy the flight of the birds who hunt these bluffs:

- ❑ American Kestrels
- ❑ Northern Harriers
- ❑ Ravens
- ❑ Vultures
- ❑ Red-tailed Hawks
- ❑ Black-shouldered Kites

Monarch Butterflies

You most certainly will see Monarch Butterflies flitting about the bluffs during the winter months. Known by their cheery reddish-orange wings edged in black, Monarchs congregate by the hundreds in the eucalyptus grove just south of the old Arleta Park train depot. A seeping spring provides water for the Monarchs, and the eucalyptus flowers nectar.

Poplar Beach offers long rolling waves, deserted broad beaches and some of the highest bluffs on Half Moon Bay.

A Walk along the Beach

The beach from Kelly Avenue to Miramontes Point is spectacular—broad, golden and generally deserted. Here you can watch long rolling breakers come ashore; you can explore the foot of sheer, 100-foot-high bluffs which enclose deep gorges; and you can find shell fragments embedded in old blue-gray rock which was once sea floor. At Miramontes Point tiny beaches and rocky tidepools beckon you to linger. Remember that the beach access from Miramontes Point parking lot is extremely dangerous. Unless you are part goat, it is best to use the Poplar Beach access trail and walk the three-quarters mile to the point.

Green Flash

Count yourself lucky if you see the famous green flash at sunset. It looks like a green flashbulb flaring on the horizon just as the last bit of sun disappears, and it is over in the blink of an eye. Conditions have to be perfect. You have to be standing at sea level and the air must be crystal clear. Old sea hands figure they will see about a dozen green flashes in their lifetime. We have seen three in fifteen years, where the sky meets the water, on Half Moon Bay.

Helpful Books

General

The Natural History of Año Nuevo edited by Burney J. Le Boeuf and Stephanie Kaza. Boxwood Press.

The Natural History of the San Francisco Bay Area by J.C. Williams and H.C. Monore. McCutchan.

The Natural History of the San Francisco Bay Region by Arthur C. Smith. University of California Press.

Sea Lions, Sea Bears and Beach Pancakes by Roger Nelson. Out of print. Available at Half Moon Bay Library.

Ocean Shore Railroad

Granada, A Synonym for Paradise: The Ocean Shore Railroad Years by Barbara VanderWerf. Gum Tree Lane Books.

Plants

A Field Guide to Pacific States Wildflowers by Theodore F. Niehaus and Charles L. Ripper. Houghton Mifflin.

Native Shrubs of the San Francisco Bay Region by Roxana S. Ferris. University of California Press.

Plants of the Coast Redwood Region by Kathleen Lyons and Mary Beth Cooney-Lazaneo. Looking Press.

Birds, Reptiles and Mammals

Birds of North America by Chandler S. Robbins, Bertel Bruun and Herbert S. Zim. Golden Press.

Handbook of California Birds by Vinson Brown, Henry Weston, Jr, and Jerry Buzzell. Naturegraph.

Water Birds of California by Howard L. Cogswell. University of California Press.

Reptiles and Amphibians of the San Francisco Bay Region by Robert C. Stebbins. University of California Press.

Mammals of the San Francisco Bay Region by William D. and Elizabeth Berry. University of California Press.

Weather and Shoreline Erosion

Weather of the San Francisco Bay Region by Harold Gilliam. University of California Press.

Living With the California Coast edited by Gary Griggs and Lauret Savoy. Duke University Press.

Gum Tree Lane Books
Celebrates the San Mateo County Coast

Granada, A Synonym for Paradise:
The Ocean Shore Railroad Years by Barbara VanderWerf
[208 pages. 128 historical and recent photos. 3 aerial photos. 21 maps. 35 line illustrations. Bibliography. Index. ISBN: 0-9632922-0-X]

"I read *Granada, A Synonym for Paradise* with much interest and pleasure. ...a substantial job of researching a remarkably intriguing place, and [written] with grace and energy."
John R. Stilgoe, Harvard University

"The [Daniel H.] Burnham dream for El Granada versus what was built is like an award-winning movie script that never made it to the screen. ...a pillar of architecture left his mark on the small town of El Granada. ...a carefully documented [account]"
Bradley Inman, *San Francisco Examiner*

"*Granada, A Synonym for Paradise*...is worthy of notice. ...it is an invaluable source...the author writes extensively on the Ocean Shore Railroad..."
Harre W. Demoro, *San Francisco Chronicle*

"...a rich account...given immediacy and color by the liberal use of quotations from old newspapers, letters, essays and novels."
Matthew Brady, *San Francisco Independent*

"...more than just a regional history of California's small coast town of El Granada: it's an exploration of common railroad myths and realities which offers invaluable, detailed insights on early railroad growth. This volume tells what it was like to live on the San Mateo coast in the early 1900s, liberally peppering its story with vintage black and white photos. Fine, simple maps, chronologies, and community insights make for a handsome result: a probe of the Ocean Shore Railroad's history and its importance to the region. Few such titles offer the solid look, research, and appeal...it's highly recommended as a unique community and landscape history."
Diane Donovan, *Bookwatch, The Midwest Book Review*

Montara Mountain:
- *San Pedro Valley County Park* • *McNee Ranch State Park*
- *Devil's Slide* • *Trails* • *Plants* • *Wildlife* • *Historical Lore*
- *San Mateo County Coast* by Barbara VanderWerf

[176 pages. Photos, maps, sketches. ISBN: 0-9632922-2-6]

"…captures the intrigue of Montara Mountain, detailing not only the great trails for hiking and biking, but also the history, the flora and the wildlife. There could be no tougher critic for such a book than myself…but VanderWerf makes it work. …a friendly relaxed style that is full of detail. She explains virtually everything about the area that fascinates so many people.

Tom Stienstra, *San Francisco Examiner*

"…describes this unique 'plant island' and the history of human settlement…well-supplied with sketches and descriptions of plants and animals. Most enjoyable are the old photos…"

Beth Geisma, *Loma Prietan,* Sierra Club

" A wonderful walk on a mountain! Bravo, VanderWerf!"

Rick Eymer, San Mateo *Times*

"It's not often a book is devoted to one mountain…offers hikes, details of plants, wildlife and interesting bits of history.

Bill Sunderland, *San Jose Mercury News*

"…celebrates pristine, biodiverse parklands in the midst of the Peninsula." Don DeNevi, *Los Altos Town Crier*

The Coastside Trail Guidebook:
- *Plants* • *Animals* • *Historical Lore*
- *Half Moon Bay*
- *San Mateo County Coast* by Barbara VanderWerf

[112 pages. Photos, maps and sketches. ISBN: 0-9632922-3-4]

"…does a marvelous job of presenting the Coastside…"

Steve Tracy, *Half Moon Bay Review*

"Don't leave home without this remarkably all-inclusive book."

Rick Eymer, San Mateo *Times*

"…a handy guide easy to bring along on any stroll…

Beth Geisma, *Loma Prietan,* Sierra Club

Order Information

To order, please send check or money order to—

Gum Tree Lane Books
P.O. Box 1574
El Granada, CA 94018

Montara Mountain	$12.95
CA sales tax (CA residents only)	1.06
Total	$14.01
The Coastside Trail Guidebook	$10.95
CA sales tax (CA residents only)	.89
Total	$11.84
Granada, A Synonym for Paradise	$15.95
CA sales tax (CA residents only)	1.32
Total	$17.27

Please add $2.50 shipping and handling for the first book ordered
and $.50 for each additional title ordered.

✄

Order form:

Title(s) _____ $ _____ . _____

_____ $ _____ . _____

_____ $ _____ . _____

CA sales tax (CA residents only) _____ $ _____ . _____

Shipping and handling _____ $ _____ . _____

Total enclosed_____ $ _____ . _____

Shipping address (please print)—

Name_____

Address_____

City_____

State_____ ZIP _____

❧

More reviews—
Granada, A Synonym for Paradise:
The Ocean Shore Railroad Years

"VanderWerf takes pride in her community and that pride shines brightly as she describes how El Granada came to be. ...[she] obviously took great pains to present an accurate account. It's worth a look."
Rick Eymer, San Mateo *Times*

"People asking about the unusual reality of small villages dotting the San Mateo coastline can have their questions answered by VanderWerf's new book. ...chock-full of historical photographs and first-person anecdotes about the San Mateo County coast."
Chris Hunter, *Pacifica Tribune*

"To VanderWerf, the history of El Granada and the railroad are inextricably linked. ...[her] fascination extends to what the railroad left behind—the old homes, the remnants of the railroad, the groves of blue gum eucalyptus and Monterey cypresses."
Marc DesJardins, *Half Moon Bay Review*

"Delightful stories, poems and pictures on every page...for anyone interested in the history of the Coastside."
Alice Jamieson, San Mateo County Historical Association

"The Ocean Shore line was so influential in developing the area that much of the book is devoted to it. ...I enjoyed the entire book."
Bob Brown, *Narrow Gauge and Short Line Gazette*

"...fascinating account of a railroad built on the dreams of real estate barons and gone in a fraction of time. At $15.95 this is a bargain."
Arthur L. Lloyd, *Western Railroader*

"...highly readable. ...well researched and crafted. ...highly recommended for anyone interested in either railroad history or 'landscape history' or both. READ IT!"
Richard Mitchell, *Ferroequinologist*